Yale Studies in English   *Richard S. Sylvester, Editor*   *Volume 166*

Vision and Judgment in Ben Jonson's Drama

by Gabriele Bernhard Jackson

New Haven and London, Yale University Press, 1968

Copyright © 1968 by Yale University.
Designed by Sheila L. de Bretteville,
set in Linotype Garamond type,
and printed in the United States of America by
The Carl Purington Rollins Printing-Office of
the Yale University Press, New Haven, Connecticut.
Distributed in Canada by McGill University Press.

Library of Congress catalog card number: 68–13912

For my father, Ernest G. Bernhard

Acknowledgments

In its original form, this book was presented as a doctoral dissertation at Yale University. To Louis Martz I am indebted for the subject, and so for the pleasures of it. Less directly, but no less surely, I owe to Martin Price's teaching the mode of thought which produced much of Chapter 4 and influenced my entire approach to Jonson's language. The writing of the study was made possible by a Sterling Fellowship, and the preparation of the manuscript in its final form was generously underwritten by Wellesley College.

To my husband, Thomas H. Jackson, for his critical suggestions solicited at last by one who detests criticism, I owe the very special gratitude attaching to rescue at the penultimate hour and the solace of taking it for granted.

The original version of this study was directed by Eugene M. Waith. I wrote for him at that time an acknowledgment of his role, and I hope he will accept its public repetition now:

Sir,

There bee many in this age, *Professors:* it does lack *Understanders.* They professe to know, by Surmises: they doe comprehend, in their sleepe. Through the shutte windore, in their closet, they examine the Sunne, if he be bright, or no. They doe drinke in *Knowledge* no quicker, at the eares; then it spews forth againe untasted. I spoke to one of eagles: he answered, cuckoo. As for such, if they will commend this worke, so, if not, let them seeke elsewhere: I am not their *Instructor.*

Yet have I seene one or two, who professe the *Faith:* they doe follow after *Truth.* Shee is not so coy a Mistresse, that shee will not reveale her selfe to a true Lover. Yet doth Gentilitie forbidde, that shee smile upon her Petitioners, in the publicke street: shee doth withdraw her selfe, to the closet of her *Understander.* In that place, Sir, I have both sought and founde her. There I have seene the Rule, by which I would be measured. Against your Understanding my worke has beene placed: you knowe mee, where I doe exceede, and where fall short. And as men doe at last perceive, they measure best, by that which is straightest; so by that Measure, Sir, I am content to be judged.

G. B. J.

Contents

Abbreviations Used in the Text and Notes

Introduction

To read Jonsonian drama is to come immediately and repeatedly upon the distinction between things as they are and things as they should be and to witness over and over the ritual of converting the one into the other. The distinction is a commonplace of satirical literature; the ritual is not. Conceiving of himself as a teacher, Jonson insisted upon following up his·lecture by taking all the examinations and duly awarding himself the degree while the audience watched.

This peculiar metamorphosis of real into ideal is possible because in Jonson's drama what is ideal has, unrecognized, been present all along. In satire it is, of course, constantly implied by techniques—imagery, ironies of action, outright comment—which Jonson used himself. But in a Jonsonian play the ideal is not only adumbrated; it is actually there. Jonson embeds it in the framework of the drama, in the principles which determine the progress and outcome of all action, in that basic structure which, in his plays, is absolutely consistent, irrespective of individual plot. Jonson saw his structural principles as analogues of the metaphysical principles which regulate the universe, in whose existence he firmly believed. The gap between real and ideal action being caused, in his view, by ignorance of these principles, he had only to clarify them for his characters and audience in order to transform the situation. As in the classroom, what should really be the case is achieved when everyone present understands what should really be the case. Rather than satirical drama, Jonson's genre might justly be called drama of revelation.

Jonson wrote drama of revelation as a matter of conviction. His deliberate choice rested on his view of the proper role of the poet— both as creator and as member of society. Accordingly, this study of his dramas begins with an investigation into his concept of poets and poetry, drawn largely from the *Discoveries* and substantiated, as well as shaded and complicated, by the series of poet-figures in his plays. That distinction between, and union of, real and ideal which occupies Jonson's drama occupies his thought about poetic composition as well. As theorist and as creator he sees double. The components of this doubleness I have called "vision" and "judgment," terms, I hope, sufficiently broad to include a spectrum of meanings without losing the capacity to illuminate. They express a distinction which I have tried in this study to trace from his poetic theory through his structural practice to his choice of specific dramatic actions and his use of language (allotting each of these one chapter). For example, in a version of this distinction, Jonson's perfect poet is simultaneously visionary and judge—superhuman seer and public man of action. At the same time, he is visionary and judge in a different sense, for Jonson equates inspiration with vision and aesthetic technique with judgment. Again, the poet as playwright is visionary and judge when he creates on the one hand an imitation of celestial truths and on the other a morally lucid depiction of human faults. Jonson's own drama presents vision in the framework and judgment in the specific content, while at the end judgment on the characters turns into vision by them. Jonson's audience, too, is included in the central dichotomy. He sees them as having an instinctive moral and aesthetic responsiveness which is analogous to the poet's faculty of vision and which grasps the poet's non-logical devices of action and language, by which the audience, in turn, is enabled to judge rightly both characters and framework. The transmission of absolute truths thus depends upon an unbroken chain of alternating vision and judgment: the poet as visionary perceives what is ultimately true; by the use of his aesthetic judgment he constructs a play the total working of which (composed of framework-vision and content-judgment) will constitute a vision—that is, a revelation—for his audience; his audience apprehends this revelation through its own faculty of ethical and aesthetic vision (which enables it to make appropriate judgments on the action); having apprehended it, the audience is to judge its own behavior against the perceived vision. Recognizing this long and relatively complicated causal chain entails, I think, reevaluating the meanings of Jonson's "didacticism," "realism," and "classicism" (which is a kind of realism), and such reevaluation is a by-product of the following discussion.

This discussion moves from the general to the particular, from large constructs to small details. In the first chapter I have illustrated and qualified Jonson's theoretical utterances about the poet by adducing his particular dramatic representations of poets, and in subsequent chapters I have examined his poetic practice as an example of his own theory—first through his overall principles of construction, then through his treatment of kinds of action, and finally through his manipulation of words. The intent is to clarify the purpose of what might appear to be less and less obviously significant parts of Jonson's dramas, as the establishment of a pattern of thought clarifies its subdivisions. The movement from constructs to details is also, as it happens, a movement from Jonson's devices for conveying his vision to his devices for conveying the judgment which depends for validation upon that initial vision. At the same time it is a movement from poet toward audience, from contemplation to communication, for the devices examined imply ever greater reliance upon ever more subtle concepts of audience response. I have tried, as the problems involved in poetic communication became more and more immediately relevant to the discussion, to investigate both *what* Jonson's choice of action and language implies about his own thought and *how* it conveys his attitudes. It is plain, therefore, that I have really dealt in every chapter with both vision and judgment, in the sense of underlying idea and aesthetic technique.

After analyzing as precisely as possible in the first chapter what Jonson meant by "poet" and "poetry," and so establishing the basic dichotomy and union between vision and judgment, I have gone on in Chapter 2 to look at his vision of universal truths as they are reflected in the "universals" of his plays. This chapter examines the implications of Jonson's single thematic pattern, of his principles of naming, his plot construction, his choice of settings—and his characters' choice of settings. Chapters 3 and 4 are concerned with Jonson's techniques for gaining acceptance of his vision: his devices of ethical "revelation," engineered to activate alogical aesthetic and ethical responses in his audience. I have chosen as examples, first, devices utilizing behavior—reactions to nobility of birth, use of money, invention and playing of games—all of which frequently recur in the dramas. In Chapter 4 I have taken up examples of verbal devices—key words, imagery, puns, alliteration.

The conclusion of this study attempts very briefly to sum up the significance, both as strength and as weakness, of Jonson's simultaneous devotion to vision and judgment. To do this I have sketched in the fluctuating relationship between the two and the rise and fall of Jonson's devotion to each, from the beginning to the end of his career. This curious interrelationship is certainly the basis of his greatness as well as the source of his greatest flaws. While his judgment on human behavior imprisons his vision of human potential in the realms of theory, that vision frees its companion judgment to transcend forever the simplistic aridity of cynicism.

1. Asper-Criticus-Quintus-Horatius-Flaccus-Jonson

"No, you starv'd rascall . . . you must have three or foure suites of
names . . . you must be call'd Asper, and Criticus, and Horace, thy
tytle's longer a reading then the stile a the big Turkes—Asper,
Criticus, Quintus Horatius Flaccus."

Dekker, *Satiromastix,* I.2.373–80

"O rare Ben Jonson!" is an exclamation of delight that breaks
seldom from the compressed lips of his critics. O learned Ben Jonson,
they chorus; O hard-working Ben Jonson; O cantankerous, O unromantic,
O fat Ben Jonson; O un-Shakespearean Ben Jonson; O arrogant and
biting Ben Jonson; but in the end (with whatever apologies), O rather
dull Ben Jonson. They refer, in their judgment, to his plays; his lyrics
can be granted felicity and, above all, influence. "The reputation of
Jonson," T. S. Eliot remarks,

> has been of the most deadly kind that can be compelled upon the
> memory of a great poet. To be universally accepted . . . to be afflicted
> by the imputation of the virtues which excite the least pleasure . . .
> this is the most perfect conspiracy of approval . . . No critic has suc-
> ceeded in making him appear pleasurable or even interesting.[1]

Yet T. S. Eliot calls Jonson a great poet, and he is speaking of Jonson's
dramas. In the mid-twentieth century, when it can be accurately re-

1. T. S. Eliot, "Ben Jonson," in *Elizabethan Essays* (London, 1934),
p. 65.

marked that aesthetic terminology has been so turned about that painters are called poets to distinguish them from the artists of other professions (artistic dignity being granted with unprecedented liberality),[2] it may not seem striking that a dramatist should be hailed as a poet, even if two of his greatest productions are in prose; but in Jonson's century and for some time thereafter, the claim was neither customary nor acceptable without further justification. It was a rare claim, and it was rare in Ben Jonson to make it. It was unprecedented in him to publish his plays in folio in 1616, entitling them *Works* and equipping them with Latin mottoes, quite as if they were serious productions instead of a collection of stage pieces which might expect "a reputation not much higher than collections of comic strips command at present"[3]—or, perhaps, of television scripts. The folio was considered by contemporaries, as it is sometimes still considered by critics, "a bit of pomposity"; the Latin mottoes, usually reserved for serious works, "a quaint flourish."[4] But this flourish

2. See Nigel Dennis, "The Seeming Truth" (review of a production of *The Merchant of Venice*), *Encounter, 14,* No. 6 (1960), 57.

3. John J. Enck, *Jonson and the Comic Truth* (Madison, 1957), p. 45.

4. Ibid., pp. 16, 45. Cf. the comments the Folio provoked at the time:

> *To Mr. Ben Johnson demanding the reason*
> *why he call'd his playes works.*

> Pray tell me *Ben,* where doth the mystery lurke,
> What others call a play you call a worke.

> *Thus answer'd by a friend in Mr. Johnson's*
> *defence.*

> The authors friend thus for the author sayes,
> *Bens* plays are works, when others works are plaies.

as well as Suckling's arhythmic recapitulation in *Fragmenta Aurea,* 1646:

> The first that broke silence was good old *Ben,*
> Prepar'd before with Canary wine,
> And he told them plainly he deserv'd the Bayes,
> For his were called Works, where others were but Plaies.

All the above verses are quoted in *Ben Jonson,* ed. C. H. Herford and Percy and Evelyn Simpson, *9,* 13. In subsequent references this edition (11 vols. Oxford, 1925–52) will be cited as HS.

heralded the official entry of Ben Jonson's claim to immortality as a peer
—in métier if not in skill—of Homer, of Horace, of Vergil. He was
making an assertion not so much of his own excellence as of the dignity
and stature of his craft, as he had done nine years earlier in his epistle
dedicatory "To The Most Noble And Most AEquall Sisters The Two
Famous Universities For Their Love And Acceptance Shewn To His
Poeme In The Presentation."[5] To call a drama a poem was sufficiently
extraordinary still to draw comment nearly a century and a half later:
" 'Tis observable that Jonson calls himself here a *poet*," remarks James
Upton in 1749, "and his plays, *poems;* making use of expressions im-
porting dignity and honour."[6] And after the passage of almost two
hundred years more, a modern editor speaks of the dedication as "a most
striking document" and points out that "the calling the play a poem is in
itself significant."[7]

   In order to estimate the significance and seriousness of Jonson's assertion, it is essential to know precisely what was being asserted. What
were the special qualities of a poet that Jonson wished to claim as his
own? Why did he not call himself a playwright, a playwright extraordinary if he wished, even a playwright unique? What things apart
were poets and poetry, that he would make himself an object of ridicule
for his contemporaries in order to affirm kinship with the socially un-
helpful ancients?

   "*A Poet* is that, which by the Greeks is call'd . . . a Maker, or a fainer
. . . not hee which writeth in measure only; but that fayneth and formeth
a fable, and writes things like the Truth" *(D,* 2347–54). These are the
two essential qualities of a poet, according to Jonson, and it is these that

---

   5. Ben Jonson, dedication to *Volpone,* reproduced from 1616 Folio in
HS, 5, 16 (spelling corrected to that of 1609 Quarto in accordance with
footnotes on p. 16). All future quotations from Jonson's works will be
taken from this edition, and the references given in abbreviated form—in
the text wherever practicable. In the spelling of such quotations, i and j
have been normalized, along with u and v.

   6. James Upton, *Remarks on Three Plays of Benjamin Jonson* (London,
1749), p. 2.

   7. Ernest Rhys, ed., *Ben Jonson* (New York, 1915), p. 17.

the following pages will elucidate and follow as determinants of his
dramatic work: to make a fable and to make it like the Truth. This is
the poet's peculiar skill, for not every man can know the truth or, having
known it, communicate it; it is his *raison d'être,* his justification for
the making of fables (for not every fable is worthwhile), his contribution
to his fellowmen and society; it is his obligation, for to be able to speak
the Truth and to keep silent is not only deceit but betrayal of oneself
and the Truth.

There was no doubt in Jonson that there was a Truth, absolute and
divine, which could be apprehended at least in part, seen in glimpses if
not in its entirety, and reproduced—not, of course, in its own form, but
in a form which would mirror it. Therefore that form must be polished
until it yielded a reflection as perfect, as nearly undistorted, as might be,
of things as they are—not as we perceive them ordinarily, but as they
exist independent of human opinion: the *Ding an sich.* The Kantian
phrase might be anachronistic, except that Jonson perfectly anticipated
it in his own explanation of the need for that exactitude of expression
which he so admired and strove to attain, not from affectation or pedantry,
but because:

> The shame of speaking unskilfully were small, if the tongue onely
> thereby were disgrac'd: But . . . disordered speech is not so much injury
> to the lips that give it forth, as to the disproportion, and incoherence
> of things in themselves, so negligently expressed. *(D,* 2135–42)

This confidence in the existence of things in themselves is quite un-
abashedly metaphysical and religious; it is referred to in metaphysical and
religious terms throughout the *Discoveries,* Jonson's most compendious
statement of his theories and beliefs, both critical and ethical. His language and the dramas he constructs of it are meant to mirror not only,
not even primarily, his age and society, but the eternal scheme of things.
The absurdity of calling Jonson a realist, in any sense other than that of a
man able to imitate real speech, becomes more and more manifest as one
begins to comprehend his vision of life and his means of communicating
it—unless one is willing to call him a realist in a more exalted sense, a
portrayer of what he believed to be the true and absolute Reality. It

would be more valid to call him a Christian Platonist, though this seems
irrelevant. It is sufficient, but it is also necessary, to understand that he
had a distinct concept of a divine order of ideal things, existing independent of, although accessible to, human comprehension, and that he
regarded himself, together with all users of "true" language, as the ex-
plicator of this order. The care which he devoted to the construction of
a play was not only a care for grace, for wit, for dramatic precepts, but a
care to make his creation "like the Truth," to enable the spectators to
see what he himself had seen. His aim was to make his ideas and their
expression neither arbitrary nor whimsical:

> The conceits of the mind are Pictures of things, and the tongue is
> the Interpreter of those Pictures. The order of Gods creatures in them-
> selves, is not only admirable, and glorious, but eloquent; Then he who
> could apprehend the consequence of things in their truth, and utter
> his apprehensions as truly, were the best Writer, or Speaker.
>
> *(D, 2128–33)*

"Truth" and "eloquence," along with "Nature," are key words in the
Discoveries. Jonson was no adherent of the Platonic dictum that art is
the imitation of an imitation; to him "things in their truth" could be
imaged in the mind without distortion. This he believed to be the
peculiar privilege of the artist. His view of art leaned heavily on the
basically Aristotelian concept of a Nature struggling to perfection but
clogged by matter. The perfection was a pre-existent pattern, the
Truth to which the Poet owed his allegiance; Nature consisted of those
forces which strove to arrange matter according to the pattern. God
was the author of the pattern, the great Orderer; but the poet was the
mortal orderer, the co-worker of Nature. "Without Art, Nature can ne're
bee perfect; &, without Nature, Art can clayme no being" *(D, 2503–04)*.
The fundamental idea is familiar, but always striking; there is something
heroic about the artist lifting his hands to release the form from the
stone, whether his tool be the chisel or the sharp-edged word.

The writing of poetry depends, then, upon a special vision—for
Jonson, a vision ethical and moral. His assertion of "the impossibility of

any mans being the good Poet, without first being a good man,"[8] is not a blow in favor of the clean life and the clear head, but a simple statement of what to him was fact. The good poet was the man who could best reproduce "the consequence of things in their truth." He must have a comprehension of the divine order; the divine order is in its nature good; therefore it follows inevitably that the man able to apprehend it must be a good man, one who shapes his mind to resemble a good order. He is "the interpreter, and arbiter of nature, a teacher of things divine, no lesse then humane" (Epistle Dedic. to *V*, 27–28).

The craft of poetry itself Jonson considered in part almost a form of divination, in part the logical and aesthetic work and skill of clothing the divined and the divine in words. A great deal of what has often been regarded as Jonson's conceit, as his arrogant enunciation of his own superiority, is more justly and more sensibly interpretable as his continuous attempt to win for poetry a recognition of its natural place, from which, through the inferiority of many of its so-called practitioners and the lack of understanding of a large part of its audience, it had sunk in the minds of men. The true poet was a moral explorer and leader, and "*Poesy* is . . . the Queene of Arts: which had her Originall from heaven, received thence from the *'Ebrewes,* and had in prime estimation with the *Greeks,* transmitted to the *Latines,* and all Nations, that profess'd Civility" *(D,* 2381–85). Poetry is, in fact, a sign of continued connection between earth and heaven—one channel of communication still preserved in a decaying, corrupt, and forgetful world. All nations that have pretended to a culture, to genuine civilization, have enlightened their darkness with fire from this torch as it passed from hand to hand. "The Study of it . . . offers to mankinde a certaine rule, and Patterne of living well, and happily; disposing us to all Civill offices of Society" *(D,* 2386–88).

Civilization, in short, depends to some considerable degree upon poetry and the knowledge obtained through that art; the state of a civilization can be judged by the status of poetry within it. Jonson considered the place of poetry in his society deplorable; in the low estimation

8. Epistle Dedicatory to *Volpone,* 22–23. The idea expressed by Jonson goes back to Strabo, *Geog.* 1.2.5, but in Jonson it has a special interpretation and significance.

in which he saw true poetry held by all but a very few, he found corroboration for his belief that the world was in a condition of progressive decay.[9] The majority neglected the "Patterne" and lived neither well nor happily. Only, as in all ages, "the wisest and best learned have thought her [Poesie] the absolute Mistresse of manners, and neerest of kin to Vertue" (D, 2394–96). But the wisest and best learned were few, and not always those with most power to reward the poet and reform his audience. Those days in which the wisest and best learned ruled, when poetry flourished and men of letters were considered the ornaments of the state, were to Jonson the last days of the world's health and the last days of any civilization worthy of the name. As the modern critic deplores the sterility of the twentieth century and yearns for the spontaneous fertility of artistic production that to him characterizes the Elizabethan Age, so Jonson mourned the materialism of the Elizabethans and yearned for the intimations of immortality granted in that pure childhood of the world, the days of the ancients.

But his classicism was far more than nostalgia for better times. He was, of course, one of the most learned and exact scholars of his day, referring constantly to the ancients in his plays and even basing whole dramas and parts of dramas on classical writings, to the scorn of many of his contemporaries, who considered him plodding, and the dismay of many of his present-day readers, who are forced to keep varied selections from the Loeb Classical Library open beside them. One of his editors, emerging from the sea of classical adaptation and allusion in which he had been submerged while grappling with the text of Poetaster, expressed in more colorful language than most the doubt which has sometimes overtaken Jonson's readers as to the real significance of his learning: "The spirit of true classicism, zoned with the cestus of beauty, her palpitant bosom defended by the aegis of law, her brow exalted and profound, had this spirit yielded up the heart of her mystery of him?"[10] Had it indeed? And was it the heart of her mystery for which Jonson was searching?

9. For allusions to this belief, which recur throughout the Discoveries, see for example lines 127, 274–80, 301–05, 921, 1380–89.

10. Herbert S. Mallory, ed., Poetaster, Yale Studies in English, 27 (New York, 1905), vi.

The rhetorical-editorial question presents, cloaked in the purple folds of language, one of the commonest misconceptions about the object of Jonson's classical studies: that he wanted to unbind the cestus of beauty, knock aside the aegis of law, and clasp classicism as his very own. The question assumes that he wished to tread in the very footsteps of Plato and Aristotle and to arrive at the same goal; that, because he named the ideal poet of his drama Horace, he wished himself to assume the toga and stand forth as the Elizabethan Horace; or that, because he quoted the doctrines of Aristotle, he wished to assume that critic's voice and pass for the Aristotle of London. But he wanted nothing of the sort. "Let *Aristotle,* and others have their dues; but if wee can make farther Discoveries of truth and fitnesse then they, why are we envied?" *(D,* 2101–03).

The most important phrase here is "Discoveries of truth." The ancients were of value to Jonson because they had revealed a portion of that abiding order to which poetry linked the fluctuating order here on earth. What they had learned and given to the world had already been tested by time and subsequent experience: it had established its authority as genuine insight. Bearing in mind Jonson's concept of the special ability and function of the poet, one can comprehend his view of the development of poetry: the building up of a body of true insight truly stated. The writings of the ancients were a precious store of knowledge, that portion of the divine scheme which man had so far succeeded in making intelligible to the human mind. When Jonson appealed to the ancients he was appealing to established truth. When he set a play in Augustan Rome, where poets ranked second only to the Emperor, he was appealing to a time in which poetry—and thus Truth—had its rightful share in government, in the very maintenance of civilization. The outcome of such a play must be regarded as valid, its judgments righteous, because the framework of the play was by definition righteous and valid. As for Jonson himself, he was to be seen not as the Elizabethan Horace but as a modern analogy: a poet with the privilege and obligation, because of his special abilities, to add to the body of truth available to mankind. Thus he entitled his collection of literary and ethical dicta *Discoveries,* or *Explorata,* and not "inventions," for he believed himself to be uncovering something which already existed, albeit something which man had perhaps not seen before. Justifying his motto in which he called himself *explorator,* he took his place with the writers of the past who had planted a standard on uncultivated territories of knowledge and claimed them for the sovereignty of man. But he did not feel that his equipment must be exactly the same as that of his predecessors; his methods might vary, his path might diverge from theirs. He explored according to the compass of his own understanding, not an imitation of theirs:

> For to all the observations of the *Ancients,* wee have our owne experience: which, if wee will use, and apply, wee have better meanes to pronounce. It is true they open'd the gates, and made the way, that went before us; but . . . Truth lyes open to all; it is no mans *severall.* . . . I doe not desire to be equall to those that went before; but to have my reason examin'd with theirs, and so much faith to be given them, or me, as those shall evict . . . if I have any thing right, defend it as Truth's, not mine. *(D,* 134–56)

In these words Jonson claimed his part in the revelation of the essential, unchanging, discoverable truth—the artistic process in each man and over generations.

A noble profession, poetry, according to Jonson; and as always, noblesse oblige. The duties of a poet are not so much aesthetic as moral; or rather, they are aesthetic insofar as the aesthetic implies the moral. That which is aesthetically most sound is that which best conveys the morally sound. In a poet "wee doe not require . . . meere *Elocution;* or an excellent faculty in verse; but the exact knowledge of all vertues, and their Contraries; with ability to render the one lov'd, the other hated, by his proper embattaling them" *(D,* 1038–41). His proper embattaling them is the poet's application of his aesthetic taste and skill; but aesthetic taste and skill are of no value except when they are turned to the service of Truth. The poet who is capable of genuine moral vision and neglects it in favor of the well-turned phrase or the apt adjective is, in Jonson's eyes, betraying his trust. Because he is in one sense superior to other men, the poet becomes in another sense their servant—in the same sense in which a king who rules by divine right is the servant of his subjects. Jonson himself implicitly makes the equation: "And, hence it is, that the comming up of good Poets . . . is so thinne and rare among us; Every beggerly Corporation affoords the State a *Major,* or two *Bailiffs,* yearly: but, *solus Rex, aut Poeta, non quotannis nascitur"* (D, 2429–34).

Just as the king's kingship is inherent in him, a grace of God and nature, so the poet's poet-ship is an inner quality, for which no amount of learning and practice will substitute. Jonson's contempt for the poet-asters of his day is the contempt of the born aristocrat for the *parvenu's* freshly painted crest. It is the contempt of Richard the Second for the usurper Bolingbroke, although Jonson would never have wished to see himself equated with a man who had so flagrantly misused his powers. For the poet, like the king, is strictly accountable to nature and to God.

But we must move from the theoretical to the practical if we wish to see the poet at his work, the lamp beside him, the paper before him, actually engaged in discovering the Truth. He has a volume of Aristotle propped against his lamp, a copy of Quintilian on his lap, Horace on the floor beside his chair; Homer he has recently reread, and rendered Vergil's description of a sea storm into three different kinds of English meter. "But all this in vaine, without a naturall wit, and a Poeticall nature in chief. For . . . but as he is adapted to it by Nature, he shall grow the per-fecter Writer" (D, 2518–22). Having prepared himself for the exercise of his art, therefore, he must give himself up to a greater power than his own if he is to have any subject matter. For,

as *Seneca* saith, *Aliquando secundum Anacreontem insanire, jucundum esse:* by which hee understands, the *Poeticall Rapture.* And according to that . . . of Aristotle; *Nullum magnum ingenium sine mixturâ dementiae fuit. Nec potest grande aliquid, & supra caeteros loqui, nisi mota mens.* Then it riseth higher, as by a divine Instinct, when it contemnes common, and knowne conceptions. It utters somewhat above a mortall mouth . . . and this made *Ovid* to boast:

  Est, Deus in nobis; agitante calescimus illo:
  Sedibus aethereis spiritus ille venit.
And *Lipsius,* to affirme; *Scio, Poetam neminem praestantem fuisse, sine parte quâdam uberiore divinae aurae.* (D, 2414–29)

The poet, then, is not only a man of superior powers. His powers are quite unlike those of ordinary human beings; he is a man apart. Isolated and heroic, he sees the truth and struggles, like Nature herself, to order his sluggish materials into a semblance of the divine pattern. He owes to earth an account of Heaven, and to Heaven an account of himself. As benefactor of society and one who makes possible true civilization, he bears a resemblance to Prometheus; but he works with, not against, the gods. His language must reflect his vision, yet be suited to the understanding of the men to whom he wishes to communicate what he has seen. His role is semimystical: he mediates between heaven and earth.

This is a remarkably romantic stance in which to find the Jonson by critical tradition so staid and earthbound. He has hardly been held up as an exponent of the *furor poeticus;* traditionally, his eye glances not from earth to heaven but from the gutter to the presence chamber. It is this interrelationship of Nature and the naturalistic, of realism and the Real, that needs to be investigated in Jonson's plays. The peculiar strength of Jonson is that he combines a reliance on the metaphysical, the not-quite-communicable vision, the absolute Truth and Order, with incorruptible common sense, relentless logic, an overwhelming sense of the ludicrous, and, in his language, an exactness of taste not to be bribed from its convictions by any sugar-candy reproduction of the Celestiall Regions. On the contrary, the society Jonson presents in his plays is usually far from celestial, resembling instead what he believed the society around him to be: it is decaying, corrupt, and forgetful, whether it be the Rome of Tiberius, Renaissance Venice, London on a fair-day, or the mythical self-absorbed court of Gargaphie. The portrayal of the divine order, insofar as Jonson succeeds in it, lies not in his portrayal of society but in the kinds of action and denouement which he allots to the creatures of society. The next chapters will be concerned with these matters in some detail.

For the present it suffices to note that he exempts from decay, corruption, and forgetfulness one man—the artist.[11] Again and again he

11. I shall consider as artists at this point only proper "users of eloquence," who actually produce good poetry or oratory, leaving aside for the present such special cases as Subtle in *The Alchemist,* Sir Dauphine Eugenie in *Epicoene,* and the witch in *The Sad Shepherd.*

places him against representatives of "realistic" society; the major conflict of his first four comedies turns on this opposition. It is as though, by rearranging, refining, recombining the elements of his thought, he were seeking to define for himself dramatically his convictions about poets and poetry—those convictions which eventually fix themselves in the fragments of the *Discoveries*.

Of Jonson's fictional artists, Knowell Junior is the simplest, as he is the earliest. Although we are never shown any of his poetry, we assume that it is good, partly because he is so clearly contrasted with the poetic aspirant Matthew, whose versifying consists mainly in rendering his plagiarisms of popular pieces a little worse by judicious alteration; partly because he adheres to the study of poetry without reward and without approbation; and partly on the authority of his name, which indicates that his efforts must be on the right track. His character is mainly interesting for the occasion it gives Jonson to present the case for and against poetry.

Knowell Senior, like his counterpart Lorenzo Senior in the play's Italian version, is a representative of social standards. Both versions open almost directly with the father's soliloquy, in which he admits to a period of life, when he was a student, spent

> Dreaming on nought but idle poetrie,
> That fruitlesse, and unprofitable art,
> Good unto none, but least to the professors,
> Which, then, I thought the mistress of all knowledge:
> But since, time, and the truth have wak'd my judgement,
> And reason taught me better to distinguish
> The vaine, from th'usefull learnings. (Folio, I.1.6–23)

In short, Knowell Senior has become a practical man. He knows well what Jonson knew equally well, that *"Poetry,* in this latter Age, hath prov'd but a meane *Mistresse,* to such as have wholly addicted themselves to her" *(D,* 622–24), and that "letters onely make men vile. Hee is upbraydingly call'd a *Poet,* as if it were a most contemptible *Nick-name" (D,* 280–82). No sensible, forward-looking father would want such a profession for his son; the Knowell Senior of today would suggest law school or engineering as a substitute. Poetry is all very well for undergraduates, but

a settled man can tell the difference between "usefull learnings" and such
as are in every sense "unprofitable." One of the play's major ironies is that,
while it is on the practical level that Knowell Senior knows better than
his son, he is thoroughly fooled in a series of *practical* jokes. The mundane
view of life is simply not enough; it will be outdone by the imaginative at
every turn, even if the outdoing is—as here—merely frivolous.

When the frivolity is over, the confusions explained, and judgment on
the participants in various deceptions pronounced by Justice Clement, we
are reminded that the case not only for the imagination in general but
for poetry in particular is being argued. Matthew's poetry is condemned,
and in the Italian version Lorenzo Senior, seizing on his apparent
triumph, exclaims, "you see,/ How abjectly your Poetry is ranckt,/ In
generall opinion" (Quarto, V.3.309–11). But Lorenzo Junior, indignant
and inspired, silences him with a declamation that already includes all the
aesthetic tenets most important to Jonson (I have italicized them):

> I can refell opinion, and approve
> The state of poesie, such as it is,
> *Blessed, aeternall, and most true devine:*
> Indeede if you will looke on Poesie,
> As she appeares in many, poore and lame,
> Patcht up in remnants and olde worne ragges,
> Halfe starved for want of *her peculiar foode,*
> *Sacred invention,* then I must conferme,
> Both your conceite and censure of her merrite.
> But view her in her glorious ornaments,
> *Set high in spirite with the precious taste*
> *Of sweete philosophie,* and which is most,
> Crownd with the rich traditions of *a soule,*
> *That hates to have her dignitie prophand,*
> *With any relish of an earthly thought:*
> Oh then how proud a presence doth she beare.
> Then is she like her selfe, *fit to be seene*
> *Of none but grave and consecrated eyes:*
>
> . . .

But that *this barren and infected age,*
Should set no difference twixt these empty spirits,
And a *true Poet:* then which *reverend name,*
Nothing can more adorne humanitie. (Quarto, V.3.315–43)

But does Lorenzo, for all his fervor, make quite clear the value of what he is defending? The entire speech is out of character; nothing concrete we know of him, only the abstract concept of his addiction to poetry, prepares us for his tirade. And the tirade itself is of a quality not altogether inspiring: the poetry of a set piece in defense of poetry ought to be beyond censure flawless, but there are points at which Lorenzo Junior's speech admits the suspicion that he has recently turned a piece of prose criticism into verse, and other points at which he comes perilously close to wrapping the cestus of beauty around the spirit of true poetry and defending her palpitant bosom with the aegis of law. The speech disrupts and alters the tone of the play, and it is not an alteration for the better.

These may well have been some of the considerations which presented themselves to Jonson's critical intelligence when he recast the play, and led him to omit the speech. From the dramatic point of view there was another excellent reason: a speech of praise from a character known to be prejudiced in favor of what he praises cannot carry much conviction, unless the language itself sweeps all before it. It comes as no surprise to us that Lorenzo Junior feels as he does about poetry; it comes as no surprise to his father either, and the speech cannot easily be accepted as changing that practical man's opinion, for he must have heard its like often before. The situation at the end of the Quarto *Every Man in* is, in respect to father and son, merely a recapitulation of the status quo. In the Folio, however, when Knowell Senior suggests that his son take the burning of Matthew's poetry as an emblem for his studies, the rebuttal is given not to Knowell Junior but to Justice Clement. Furthermore, it is couched in language appropriate in tone and diction both to Justice Clement and to the play as a whole:

Nay, no speech, or act of mine be drawne against such, as professe it [Poetry] worthily. They are not borne everie yeere, as an Alderman.

There goes more to the making of a good *Poet,* then a Sheriffe . . . You looke upon me! though, I live i' the citie here, amongst you, I will doe more reverence, to him, when I meet him, then I will to the Major [Mayor], out of his yeere. (V.5.37–43)[12]

These changes gain for the rebuttal two significant effects which support its authority. Its language, fitting into the language of the play, convinces us that such an utterance is indeed the natural conclusion of such an argument, that the decision is in accord with the evidence. Its assignment to Justice Clement, who, in this comedy, is the earthly and earthy representative of divine justice, lifts the conclusion out of the realm of the arguable utterance into that of the absolutely just. Justice Clement decides the final fate of every character: he sees through all deceptions, untangles all confusions, and gives to everyone justice according to his deserts. He has no personal involvement in the struggles of the protagonists; his justice is tempered only with mercy, according to his name and the precepts of religion, and with good humor, according to the precepts of Ben Jonson. Therefore, when he pronounces judgment in the dispute between father and son, his decision is, by the nature of his dramatic function, absolutely final.

The change from impassioned special pleading to cool, colloquial outside judgment also gains for young Knowell's poetic efforts a most important implication: they do appeal to the intelligent practical man. Justice Clement enlarges the scope of poetic effectiveness from the student's ivory tower to the active world, represented by him and, in his comparisons, by the City officials. Thus Knowell Senior is disqualified as genuine spokesman of society; he represents it only insofar as it is unimaginative. He brings down upon himself the explicit refutation of his views when his failure of imagination (specifically, poetic imagination) disables him from distinguishing between his son's verses and Matthew's. Justice Clement, by contrast, is more practical than old Knowell (he is not fooled by the young men's tricks) just because he is more imaginative. The balanced combination characterizes society at its best.

12. Cf. *D,* 2429–34, quoted on p. 14, above.

The place of poetry in the world of action remained centrally problematic for Jonson, in art as in life. The solution of *Every Man in*—to assert by fiat that poetry is important to the truly practical man and that he appreciates it—was cheery but inadequate. Jonson remained internally plagued by the need to find a practical justification for poetic activity and hit very soon upon the alternatives to which he clung for the rest of his life: poetry is in itself an agent of correction, and/or poetic imagination is symptomatic of all ordering imagination and therefore of the ability to rule society. The first alternative produced Jonson's view of himself as satirist, and the satirists of *Poetaster* and *Every Man out*, as well as Virgil in the former play and Crites in *Cynthia's Revels*. The second alternative produced Cicero *(C)*, Augustus *(P)*, Cynthia *(CR)*, and a galling sense of neglected personal desert.

In *Every Man in* poetic imagination as a means to social order receives a weak embodiment in Justice Clement, whose appreciation of genuine poetry is an afterthought and coexists with his fondness for rowdy doggerel. Poetry as a corrective receives no embodiment at all. The society to be ordered is simple and basically sound. There are a few incorrigible pretenders who promote falsehood and must be excluded from the banquet at the end; there are some practical men who lack imagination and must be corrected before they can eat, just as there are some over-imaginative but unpoetic minds which must be calmed; and there are Justice Clement, Brainworm, Knowell Junior, and Wellbred, all properly imaginative and therefore practically successful. But the issue of poetry is only nominally central, never entering into the main action, while imagination or vision is not mentioned and so must be deduced as an abstract criterion. Three years after the play first appeared, Jonson composed *Poetaster* and, in so doing, recomposed *Every Man in* and its overly simple picture of the poet's role. In *Poetaster* the issue of poetry is the whole concern of the plot. Society here is not merely pretentious but in the process of real corruption, and a major agent of corruption is Ovid, the poet himself.

This is by no means immediately obvious. In the first scene of the play Ovid seems merely a stronger retracing of Lorenzo-Knowell Junior. His father, going one step further than Lorenzo-Knowell Senior, has not only recommended law school to his son but actually forced him to enroll. Ovid, predictably, is by inclination and natural gifts on the side of "sacred Poesy . . . spirit of arts,/ The soul of science, and the queen of souls." Like Lorenzo Junior, he perceives the difference

> twixt those jaded wits
> That runne a broken pase for common hire,
> And the high raptures of a happy *Muse,*
> Borne on the wings of her immortall thought,
> That kickes at earth with a disdainefull heele,
> And beats at heaven gates with her bright hooves. *(P,* I.2.241–46)

Indeed, his position on the side of poetry is more convincing and commands more respect than that of Lorenzo-Knowell Junior, because we know from the beginning that Ovid has in fact written immortal verse. His a priori claims are buttressed by his recitation in Scene 1 of an elegy he has supposedly just composed, by his speaking verse throughout an opening scene in which all the other characters (attackers of poetry) speak prose, and by the information that he is so given by nature to versifying that he cannot even make notes on jurisprudence in prose: "How now OVID! *Law*-cases in verse?" exclaims his friend Tibullus, glancing at the papers on Ovid's table, and the latter replies: "In troth, I know not: they runne from my pen/ Unwittingly, if they be verse" (I.3.7–9). Clearly he is fitted by Nature to be a true poet; he lisps in numbers, for the numbers come. Not for fame (he is as yet unknown), nor for fortune (he is "a yonger brother, and hast nothing, but thy bare exhibition: which I protest shall bee bare indeed, if thou forsake not these unprofitable by-courses" [I.2.75–78]), but because it is his true vocation and he cannot help himself, Ovid becomes a poet.

The "practical" opposition he has to face is also an intensification of young Knowell's. In the same words as old Knowell, Ovid Senior objects to poetry as "Unprofitable" (I.2.77), "idle," and "fruitlesse" (I.2.139), but he is much more downright about his charges against the "meane

Mistresse": she not only keeps his son from acquiring substance, she is wasting his own:

> Are these the fruits of all my travaile and expenses? Is this the scope
> and aime of thy studies? . . . verses? *poetrie?* OVID, whom I thought
> to see the pleader, become OVID the play-maker? . . . Name me a pro-
> fest *poet,* that his *poetrie* did ever afford him so much as a compe-
> tencie. (I.2.5–9, 78–79)

With approbation, he seizes upon the description that his fellow philis-
tine, Captain Tucca, offers of Homer: "a poore, blind, riming rascall, that
liv'd obscurely up and downe in boothes, and tap-houses, and scarce ever
made a good meale in his sleepe" (I.2.84–87), and he anticipates Ovid's
objection that Homer and his works are divine, with the triumphant
question, "But could this divinitie feed him, while he liv'd? . . . or give
him . . . worship, or attendants? make him be carried in his litter?"
(I.2.91–92, 95–96)

But though poetic imagination is once again on trial, this time the
argument turns out to be far more complex. For not only is Ovid contrasted with his father and the latter's supporters, all of whom are made
ridiculous by their own vehemence, and with the poetasters Crispinus and
Demetrius, who correspond to the poetasting Matthew, but Ovid must
undergo comparison also with the poets acknowledged as greatest—
Horace and Virgil—and eventually with his own poetic ideal. It is
against these that he is weighed in the balance and found wanting. While
his father lacks the most basic poetic imagination, Ovid lacks poetic
imagination of a higher sort. He gives lip recognition, but no real understanding, to the spiritual nature of poetry. Scarcely has he finished exclaim-
ing against the lack of poetic imagination in men like his father and de-
claring that with such imagination "They would admire bright knowledge,
and their minds/ Should ne're descend on so unworthy objects,/
As gold, or titles" (I.2.249–51), when he is utterly turned from his
exalted studies by a woman's letter. True, a mistress is theoretically of
more spiritual worth than gold or titles; yet while Ovid's passion for
Julia has spiritual possibilities, it relies largely on physical actualities. Her
lustrous eye, her melodious voice, the "pure *elyzian* sweets" of her breath,

the "glories of the summer" in her looks lead him to pronounce her identical with Heaven and to dedicate his art to her (I.3.38–46). Although his friend's "PUBLIUS, thou'lt lose thy selfe," may sound a momentary ominous note for us, Ovid does not hear it. Enthusiastically he repeats his affirmations:

> JULIAS love
> Shall be a law, and that sweet law I'le studie,
> The law, and art of sacred JULIAS love:
> All other objects will but abjects proove. (I.3.55–58)

This is certainly not the Heaven with which the true poet, according to Jonson, communicates: verses to a mistress are no fulfillment of the poet's moral duty to express his vision as a pattern for true civilization. The law and art of courting a woman are not the law and art which refine a gifted man into an eloquent writer. When Ovid declares his intention to neglect all other studies for Julia's love, to depend upon his own poetical nature and Julia's inspiration for the shaping of his art, he places himself among

> the obstinate contemners of all helpes, and Artes: such as presuming on their own *Naturals* (which perhaps are excellent) dare deride all diligence ...
> *It cannot* but come to passe, that these men, who commonly seeke to doe more then enough, may sometimes happen on some thing that is good, and great; but very seldome: And when it comes, it doth not recompence the rest of their ill. *(D, 745–64)*

A hierarchy is in the making. As in *Every Man in,* appreciation of poetry is better than scorn, and poetry by a genuine poet, naturally adapted for his craft, is better than poetry by an untalented upstart. But poetry relying on inspiration alone—and, above all, on inspiration from airs so distinctly earthly as the breath of a mistress—is no equal of the poetry of Horace and Virgil, dependent on religious and ethical vision and written for the good of mankind.

The case against Ovid is worse than a charge of omission alone could render it, however. To make of an attractive woman, more perfect in beauty than in reputation, a sacred object is a profanation of the eternal verities accessible to the poet. Ovid extends the sacrilege until it becomes explicit blasphemy in the banquet at which he and his friends represent the Olympians, with Ovid as Jupiter and Julia as Juno. The banquet is central to the play, in structure as well as intention,[13] for it presents fully the failure of Ovid as the good poet and the good man.

The profane objects of this heavenly celebration are set forth in a proclamation at its beginning which leaves no room for doubt that here is no aspiration of men toward the gods, but only a debasement of divinity to the lowest and most physical level of man:

> The great God, JUPITER,
> Of his licentious goodnesse,
> Willing to make this feast, no fast
> From any manner of pleasure;
> Nor to bind any God or Goddesse
> To be any thing the more god or goddess, for their names:
> He gives them all free licence,
> . . . to be nothing better, then common men, or women,
> And therefore no God
> Shall need to keep himselfe more strictly to his Goddesse,
> Then any man do's to his wife.
> Nor any Goddesse,
> Shall need to keepe her selfe more strictly to her God,
> Then any woman do's to her husband.
> But, since it is no part of wisdome,
> In these daies, to come into bonds;
> It shall be lawfull for every lover,
> To breake loving oathes,
> To change their lovers, and make love to others,

13. Although the introduction of the banquet as a major concern of the principal characters occurs in Act IV, consideration of the play in terms of lines and scenes reveals that the description of the feast is indeed physically central. Cornelius Gallus' outline of it in IV.2.21–24 is preceded by 1612 lines of text and followed by 1607. The play is divided into 21 scenes; Gallus' outline of the banquet occurs in the middle of scene 11.

As the heate of every ones bloud,
And the spirit of our *nectar* shall inspire.
And, JUPITER, save JUPITER. (IV.5.12–34)

With a good deal of not-over-witty bawdry, the feast proceeds, and we are permitted to witness for the first time an interchange between Ovid and his sacred Julia:

OVID. Wee are a King, cotqueane; and we will raigne in our pleasures; and wee will cudgell thee to death, if thou finde fault with us.

JULI. I will find fault with thee, King cuckold-maker: . . . And there is never a starre in thy fore-head, but shall be a horne, if thou persist to abuse me. . . .

OVID. We tell thee, thou anger'st us, cot-queane; and we will thunder thee in peeces, for thy cot-queanitie. (IV.5.93–96, 121–25)

The travesty of all things spiritual, including the emotion of love, could not be more complete. Within the Roman framework of the play the religion which Ovid and his friends are ridiculing is the true religion, and their sacrilege consequently stands for blasphemy in general. Despite Ovid's poetic talent, his character is to the character of an ideal poet as Matthew's versifying is to ideal poetry: "Poetry? nay then, call blasphemie, religion;/ Call Divels, Angels; and Sinne, pietie:/ Let all things be preposterously transchangd" *(EI,* Quarto, V.3.305–07).

With such provocation, Jupiter, not too surprisingly, does not preserve "Jupiter." Now that Ovid has discredited himself privately among his companions, it remains for him to be discredited publicly among his fellow poets (just as Matthew's minor disgrace before his "mistress" is followed by Justice Clement's final condemnation of him). The Emperor, informed of the banquet by a slanderer hoping for advancement, breaks in upon the festivities and condemns the participants in lines which reinstate as accepted truths Jonson's most cherished assumptions about the role of poetry and poets:

Are you, that first the *deities* inspir'd
With skill of their high natures, and their powers,

The first abusers of their usefull light;

...

O, who shall follow vertue, and embrace her,

...

When you, that teach, and should eternize her,
Live, as shee were no law unto your lives:
Nor liv'd her selfe, but with your idle breaths?

...

As if there were no vertue, but in shade
Of strong imagination, meerely enforce't?
This shewes, their knowledge is meere ignorance;
Their farre-fetcht dignitie of soule, a phansy;
And all their square pretext of gravitie
A meere vaine-glorie. (IV.6.34–47, 68–73)

Augustus finds it necessary to uphold *"The strength* of Empire [which] is in Religion" *(D,* 1197) against the poets who should be its supporters, and to reaffirm the existence of absolute truth against the men who should be her sworn champions. It is true that beside this condemnation we must place Horace's designation of the banquet as "innocent mirth,/ And harmelesse pleasures, bred, of noble wit" *(P,* IV.7.41–42). But Horace has not heard the proclamation or the dialogue between the supposed king and queen of the gods. The audience is well aware that he has not been present at the feast and that his open, magnanimous, and forgiving nature would incline him to put upon the banquet a construction as harmless as possible, while inclining him equally or even more to despise the informer to whom he addresses his description.

Besides, it is not Horace but Virgil who emerges in the last act as the Emperor's right hand, capable of holding the scepter of the judge. In the final hierarchy even Horace must—and willingly does—yield place to the divine Virgil, whose "rectified spirit" is "refin'd/ From all the tartarous moodes of common men;/ Bearing the nature, and similitude/ Of a right heavenly bodie" (V.1.100–05); who writes "As if his mindes peece, which he strove to paint,/ Could not with fleshly pencils have her right" (V.1.114–15), so careful is he in his choice of words; and whose finished work

> Is with such judgement, labour'd, and distill'd
> Through all the needfull uses of our lives,
> That could a man remember but his lines,
> He should not touch at any serious point,
> But he might breathe his spirit out of him. (V.1.119–23)

Here is a complete embodiment of poetry's constructive social powers. In Virgil we find at last "Romes honour" (V.1.69), a man who is worthy, as earthly representative of Virtue, to take his place "Above best Kings, whom onely she should make" (V.2.26–27). He has purified his spirit to receive the divine vision and has communicated it completely as a practical benefaction. How close this brings him to Jonson's other alternative, the use of poetic imagination for the active regulation of society, can be seen in the Emperor's words:

> CAESAR, and VIRGIL
> Shall differ but in sound; to CAESAR, VIRGIL
> (Of his expressed greatness) shall be made
> A second sur-name, and to VIRGIL, CAESAR. (V.2.2–5)

Just below Virgil stands Horace, also a representative of corrective poetry, lesser not through any moral failing but simply because his poetry does not attain the heights Virgil's does. The poet cannot rise higher than his initial vision, for "wheras all other Arts consist of Doctrine, and Precepts: the *Poet* must bee able by nature, and instinct, to powre out the Treasure of his minde" *(D,* 2411–13). The treasure of Horace's mind is perhaps less copious, perhaps of slightly less precious metal, than the treasure of Virgil's. Nonetheless he does deal with the matter of true poetry and also engages actively in correcting the wrongheaded. Thus he ranks higher than Tibullus, who, like Ovid, has confinèd himself to love elegies and the cultivation of the inner man. Yet Tibullus and his fellow poet Cornelius Gallus seem to have in common with Horace, although to a lesser degree, a basic ethical soundness, which leads the Emperor to pardon them for their participation in the banquet. "You both have vertues, shining through your shapes," he tells them, and goes on to cite specifically their devotion to "Sweet *poesies* sacred garlands . . ./ Which is, of all the faculties on earth,/ The most abstract, and perfect" (*P*, V.1.13–19).

This concept of poetry as essentially nonphysical is entirely perverted by Ovid, who perceives only in physical terms. His passion for Julia leaves him primarily . interested in sweet poetry's profane garlands. Even at the final moment, as he parts from her to go into exile, he characteristically expresses himself in a punning erotic epigram: "Ay me, there is no stay/ In amorous pleasures: if both stay, both die" (IV.9.95–96). Indeed, the entire parting scene between the lovers confirms the justice of Ovid's exile from the society of worthy poets. When Julia offers to throw herself from the window in proper Sapphic tradition, Ovid dissuades her by pointing out that she will inadvertently convert herself entirely into spirit and so deprive herself of the physical pleasures which, by his definition, constitute love. This consideration takes her sufficiently aback to keep her at the window while her lover makes the lamentable situation clear:

> O, stay, my love: . . .
> . . .
>   . . . when thou art dead,
> Thou onely must survive in perfect soule;
> And in the soule, are no affections:
> We powre out our affections with our bloud;
> And with our blouds affections, fade our loves.
> . . .
> "Beautie, compos'd of bloud, and flesh, moves more,
> "And is more plausible to bloud, and flesh,
> "Then spirituall beautie can be to the spirit. (IV.9.27–41)

From a man supposedly dedicated to poetry, this is open heresy. Ovid is a weak man, morally and emotionally: his passion has overcome his original understanding of the aim and function of his art. We may recall, now that his exalted convictions have been overwhelmed, that he never quite had the courage of them. Unlike Horace, he tolerated and even encouraged Crispinus for his own amusement,[14] and despite his impassioned monologue on the subject of poetry, he speaks not one word in its defense against his father, whose scorn at its height draws forth only:

> Sir, let me crave you will, forgoe these moodes;
> I will be any thing, or studie any thing:
> I'le prove the unfashion'd body of the *law*
> Pure elegance. (I.2.103–06)

The genuine poet is a man strong enough to maintain his position in a hostile world, but Ovid cannot even stand without wavering in a world which is the epitome of friendliness and appreciation toward poetry. The opinion that "it is . . . 'the poet *contra mundum,* that it [*Poetaster*] dramatizes"[15] is a misconception fostered by the play's early scenes and the war of the theaters. *Poetaster* might be better called— availing oneself to the full of the authoritative foreign phrase—the play of the poet *cum mundo par excellence.* By the end of the play the world is so much with Ovid that he has become one of those who

> beleeve not themselves, what they would perswade others; and lesse doe the things, which they would impose on others: but least of all, know what they themselves most confidently boast. Only they set the signe of the Crosse over their outer doores, and sacrifice to their gut, and their groyne in their inner Closets. *(D, 50–55)*

We can measure his fall by the contrast between his soliloquy in Act I on the "prophane violence, almost sacriledge," that has been offered the

14. See Eugene M. Waith, "The Poet's Morals in Jonson's *Poetaster,*" *Modern Language Quarterly,* 12 (March 1951), 16.

15. Rhys, *Ben Jonson,* pp. 13–14. The question of the identification of Crispinus and Demetrius as Marston and Dekker, and of Horace as Jonson, along with all the subsidiary identifications which may or may not be valid, are omitted as irrelevant to the subject under discussion. They are treated at length by Josiah H. Penniman in *The War of the Theatres* (Boston, 1897) and by Roscoe Addison Small in *The Stage-Quarrel between Ben Jonson and the So-Called Poetasters* (Breslau, 1899).

"divinities" of poetry by those who cannot "admire bright knowledge" without the admixture of "unworthy objects" (I.2.231–51) and his final words before he goes into exile: "The truest wisdome silly men can have,/ Is dotage, on the follies of their flesh" (IV.9.108–09). From Augustan Rome, where the standards of society overcome factional philistinism as well as factional corruption and remain the standards set by poetic imagination, Ovid must be exiled, for he has betrayed his trust. Though graced with a poetic nature, he has abandoned the privileges and responsibilities of the poet in both aspects of his double role, as Seer and as benefactor of society. By the end of the play, he has no longer anything to give.

In *Poetaster,* then, Jonson dramatized what *Every Man in* had only implied: the social value of good poetry and the good poet, the practical value of imagination. He also amplified his definition of "poet" to include degrees of goodness corresponding to degrees of vision, which in turn correspond to degrees of ethical utility. Most important, however, because it is the greatest departure from his earlier position, is the parallel between Ovid and Matthew, which so quickly replaces the parallel between Ovid and young Knowell. Jonson's simple equation between bad ethics and bad poetry is gone. Poetry, it now seems, may be effective in undesirable ways. A man intended by nature for a poet may be corrupted from within yet retain his talent. This distinction between the true and the perverse artist, which is also a distinction between the socially and the privately motivated man, opens a field of action for Subtle, for Mosca, for Catiline. It closes Jonson's work forever to the appearance of another Brainworm, the man of imagination who operates harmlessly for private ends and receives applause in his success from the representative of ordered society. From *Poetaster* onward all imagination used for personal gratification becomes sinister, a force which undermines society.

Before *Poetaster* Jonson's plays presented, with little conscious ambivalence, poetic imagination as purely salutary *(EI, EO, CR)*. After *Poetaster*, as though the character of Ovid had embodied a revelation, Jonson became fascinated with the possibilities of imagination as purely poisonous *(S, V, A)*. In *Catiline* he brought the two face to face, pitted them against one another, and, having seen to it that constructive imagination thoroughly triumphed, never wrote another drama in which the imaginative orderer—or disorderer—was central. By main force, he had settled some conflict within himself between the amoral pleasures of irresponsible invention and the moral justification of responsible artistry. Having scourged, imprisoned, robbed, exiled, and executed the former in the shape of its dramatic representatives, he found he had to goad it into self-destruction before he could accept its unacceptability.

In *Catiline* the ultimate polarity between true and false artist takes form as a confrontation between two rhetoricians, one the potential destroyer and one the potential savior of civilization. Catiline and his conspirators, like Ovid and his friends, represent Rome's worst impulses: self-seeking, desire for wealth, contempt of the gods. Catiline is no mean orator; his speeches to his confederates, to his army on the point of battle, and even in the senate chamber do not lack fire or conviction. What they lack are truth and virtue. Despite his rhetorical abilities, he is never called eloquent, a word which Jonson seems to have reserved as a value judgment. Cicero's eloquence is affirmed again and again, not only by his supporter Cato (IV.472) but even by his most bitter enemies, Sempronia (II.124) and Catiline (IV.159, 470). Catiline glories in his wickedness; Cicero rests secure in his virtue, proud of his humility.

Considering the play with the same sensibilities which warm toward Milton's Satan and remain unmoved by the Almighty, we may well find Catiline the more attractive of the opponents; but there can be no question as to Cicero's function as representative of the gods and savior of Rome. At every turn he calls upon the deities to invoke their blessing or thank them for their care, while Catiline and his cohorts scoff at the divine powers, and even Caesar, who secretly sympathizes with the conspirators, is not exempted by Cato from the imputation of heresy when he advocates lifelong exile for the discovered plotters:

As if he thought those things, a prettie fable,
That are deliver'd us of hell, and furies,
Or of the divers way, that ill men goe

From good, to filthy, darke, and ugly places.
And therefore, he would have these live; and long too. (V.528–32)

As one might deduce from the even opposition between Catiline and
Cicero, so much more a genuine contest than the "opposition" between
Ovid and the ethical poets, Rome herself is in a desperate state. Civilization hangs in the balance; the strength of Catiline symbolizes Rome's own
inner corruption by power, luxury, and arrogant impiety:

Shee builds in gold; and, to the starres:
As, if shee threatned heav'n with warres:
And seekes for hell, in quarries deepe,
Giving the fiends, that there doe keepe,
A hope of day. (I.551–55)

A civilization gets the artist it deserves—as Mosca and Subtle have
previously demonstrated. But in *Catiline* Jonson reverts to a hope he
seemed to have abandoned in *Volpone* and *The Alchemist:* that even a
corrupt civilization might contain somewhere that poetic imagination
which figures the power of creative ordering. Its possessor would clearly
have to be a man apart from society's infected traditions and government,
yet he would also have to receive opportunity for social effectiveness.
Jonson therefore presents us with Cicero, the "new man," first in his
family to hold office, unexpected winner of the consular election, the
good orator and the good man.

The identification between orator and poet was an ancient one: the
Renaissance inherited from Rome the rhetorical tradition in which no
clear distinction was made between the two forms of verbal manipulation. Jonson himself considered the poet "the neerest Borderer upon
the Orator," who "expresseth all his vertues, though he be tyed more to
numbers," and who "must have *Civil prudence*" to practice "the most
prevailing Eloquence" *(D,* 2528–30, 2522–23, 2294–95). For a dramatic
demonstration of the practical utility of imagination, the orator provides
a perfect extension of the poet. Equipped with his art, he is prepared
to shape the society in which he lives.

Jonson's whole concept of the artist-ruler is well within the outlines of his basically Platonic system of thought. Plato's celebrated philosopher-king is also, but less celebratedly, an artist. Plato begins, indeed, by referring to the philosopher only: "neither cities nor States nor individuals will ever attain perfection until the small class of philosophers . . . not corrupt are providentially compelled . . . to take care of the State . . . or until kings . . . are divinely inspired with a true love of true philosophy." But as his discussion progresses, the philosopher-thinker soon merges into the philosopher-artist: "will they disbelieve us, when we tell them that no State can be happy which is not designed by artists who imitate the heavenly pattern?" Such an artist,

> holding converse with the divine order, becomes orderly and divine, as far as the nature of man allows . . . And if a necessity be laid upon him of fashioning, not only himself, but . . . States or individuals, into that which he beholds elsewhere, will he, think you, be an unskilful artificer of justice, temperance, and every civil virtue? . . . They [the artists] will begin by taking the State and the manners of men, from which, as from a tablet, they will rub out the picture, and leave a clean surface. . . . And when they are filling in the work, as I conceive, they will often turn their eyes upwards and downwards: I mean that they will first look at absolute justice and beauty and temperance, and again at the human copy; and will mingle and temper the various elements of life into the image of a man; and thus they will conceive according to that other image, which, when existing among men, Homer calls the form and likeness of God.[16]

Since the activities of Plato's ideal ruler and Jonson's ideal poet are nearly identical, it is hardly surprising that, while Plato sees his philosopher as basically an artist, Jonson sees his artist as basically a philosopher: "the wisest and best learned . . . wheras they entitle *Philosophy* to bee a rigid, and austere *Poesie:* they have (on the contrary) stiled *Poesy,* a dulcet, and gentle Philosophy, which leades on, and guides us by the

16. Plato, *The Republic,* Bk. VI, in *The Dialogues of Plato,* trans. Benjamin Jowett, 3 (3d ed. 5 vols. London, 1924), 199–200. Despite Plato's unflattering pronouncements elsewhere, he really is speaking here of *"artists who imitate the heavenly pattern"*: his word is ζωγράφοι.

hand to Action" *(D, 2394–99)*.[17] And for Jonson as for Plato, the ideal creator of an earthly government is this philosopher-artist: Jonson "could never thinke the study of *Wisdome* confin'd only to the Philosopher: or of *Piety* to the *Divine:* or of State to the *Politicke*. But that he which can faine a *Common-wealth* (which is the *Poet*) . . . is all these" *(D, 1032–38)*.

Cicero, as he is characterized in *Catiline,* might have been consciously drawn to fit this version of Plato's specifications. To the astonishment of the conspirators and all who do not understand or appreciate his spiritual qualifications, he is "providentially compelled . . . to take care of the State"; that is, he is elected to the consulship, in association with the political cipher Antonius, who is obviously incapable of lifting from Cicero's shoulders one ounce of the responsibility the consuls ought jointly to bear. Cato makes Rome's position plain as he salutes Cicero: "Our need made thee our *Consul,* and thy vertue" (III.56–57). The moment is clearly at hand for an artist to appear who can design the State according to the "heavenly pattern," one of those who "begin by taking the State and the manners of men . . . And one feature they will erase, and another they will put in, until they have made the ways of men, as far as possible, agreeable to the ways of God," for "in no way could they make a fairer picture."[18] Like Cincinnatus from his farm, the artist must come when called from his study to assume the mantle of public responsibility. Having shown himself the good man and the

17. "The wisest and best learned" in this case include Sidney. See the *Defence of Poesy,* ed. Albert S. Cook (Boston, 1890), pp. 13–32, especially the following:

> So that the ending end of all earthly learning being virtuous action, those skills that most serve to bring forth that have a most just title to be princes over the rest; wherein . . . the poet is worthy to have it before any other competitors. Among whom as principal challengers step forth the moral philosophers [p. 13] . . . I say the philosopher teacheth, but he teacheth obscurely, so as the learned only can understand him . . . But . . . the poet is indeed the right popular philosopher [p. 18]. . . . For he doth not only show the way, but giveth so sweet a prospect into the way as will entice any man to enter into it [p. 23].

18. Jowett, *Plato, 3,* 200.

good poet, "a man/ And master of thy art" (III.63–64), he must turn
that art to the practical benefit of the commonwealth, to the curing of a
sick society. He must be prepared to forsake his manuals of navigation
and guide the ship of state without book. "Each petty hand," Cato tells
Cicero,

> Can steere a ship becalm'd; but he that will
> Governe, and carry her to her ends, must know
> His tides, his currents; how to shift his sailes;
> What shee will beare in foule, what in faire weathers;
> Where her springs are, her leakes; and how to stop 'hem;
> What sands, what shelves, what rocks do threaten her;
> The forces, and the natures of all winds,
> Gusts, stormes, and tempests; when her keel ploughs hell,
> And deck knocks heaven: then, to manage her,
> Becomes the name, and office of a pilot. (III.64–74)

The real concern of the image is emphasized by the enjambment of the
first and second lines, combined with the caesura after "governe."
Control is crucially important for the artist-statesman, who must
"manage" not only his aesthetic but his political materials, in this case
his words and the people of the republic, so as to assure truth and order.
The storms and tempests exemplify nature in chaos, in and through
which order must be found; the ship whose deck knocks heaven and keel
ploughs hell is particularly apt as symbol of the Rome that builds to the
stars "As, if shee threatned heav'n with warres:/ And seekes for hell, in
quarries deepe." The equation of eloquence in action with the manage-
ment of a ship is one which seems to have struck Jonson as especially
just, probably because of its overtones of nature comprehended, her own
forces turned to man's use. At any rate, he believed like the wisest and
best learned of the Romans in his play that "it is one thing to be
eloquent in the *Schooles,* or in the *Hall;* another at the *Barre,* or in the
Pulpit . . . indeed I would no more chuse a *Rhetorician,* for reigning in a
Schoole; then I would a *Pilot,* for rowing in a *Pond*" (D, 424–25, 436–37).
But Cicero's powers extend far beyond reigning in a school, and he is a

worthy pilot for the open sea of government. His natural eloquence and
virtue, extolled throughout the play, have been polished by study: he has
"suck'd at *Athens*" *(C,* II.137). He is religious, strong in the consciousness of his power, but conscious also of the Powers above him. His fitness
for rule, like his eloquence, is natural; the ambassadors of the Allobroges,
disgusted with the Romans they have observed passing along the street,
recognize at once that Cicero and his companions (of whose identity they
are unaware) "Seeme of another race . . . / There's hope of justice, with
their fortitude" (IV.36–37). His manner strikes "an awe" into them,
and wins

> a more reguard
> Unto his place, then all the boystrous moodes
> That ignorant greatnesse practiseth, to fill
> The large, unfit authoritie it weares.
> How easie is a noble spirit discern'd . . . (IV.45–50)

Yet he is rendered fit for his authority by more than his natural qualities
and literary studies. Like every true artist, he guides himself by the
divine pattern he, but not other men, can perceive, inspiring Cato to
exclaim, "Good MARCUS TULLIUS (Which is more, then great)/
Thou had'st thy education, with the gods" (V.99–100).

There are indeed moments in the play when the manifold functions
Cicero arrogates to himself remind one of the guardian dog in *Alice in
Wonderland* addressing a troublesome mouse: " 'I'll be judge, I'll be jury,'
Said cunning old Fury; 'I'll try the whole cause, and condemn you to
death.' " But Cicero is never, after all, jury, and although he executes
the sentence when it is passed by the senators, he does not condemn to
death. On the contrary, his extreme desire to temper justice with mercy—
which leads him instead of arresting his would-be murderers to urge
them to mend their ways—makes him a true representative of divine
justice, which is also tempered with mercy. His refusal, in the absence of
conclusive evidence, to prosecute Caesar, whose guilt is plain, exemplifies
his godlike combination of justice and mercy and elicits Cato's exclamation. In respect to his fitness for judgment, the great orator is a counterpart of his lesser colleague, Justice Clement: the merciful Justice under-

stands the nature of poetry, and the poet-orator the nature of merciful justice. Both are commissioners of the justice of Heaven:

> For hee that is religious, must be mercifull and just necessarily . . .
> Justice is the vertue, that Innocence rejoyceth in. Yet even that is not
> always so safe; but it may love to stand in the sight of mercy . . . No
> vertue is a *Princes* owne; or becomes him more, then his *Clemency.*
>
> (*D,* 1200–04, 1162–63)

Cicero brings together the roles of prince, judge, and artist. In his perfect fulfillment of them all, he exceeds even Augustus, who refuses the plea to "forgive: be like the Gods" *(P,* IV.6.60). And Cicero should stand one ridge higher on Olympus than Augustus, for as artist and ruler he combines in himself Augustus, Virgil, and Horace. This is his justification for being at once accuser (Horace), judge (Virgil), and head of state (Augustus).

The situation and outcome of *Catiline* parallel those of *Poetaster* as the striking of a clock parallels the drawing of its mechanism. What in *Poetaster* is outlined as potentiality, in *Catiline* becomes action. The evil which Ovid and the poetasters represent sketchily and lightly is realized in the thoroughly corrupt and licentious Catiline and his confederates. The banishment of Catiline, redemption of such of the conspirators as can be saved, and destruction of the rest translate into the realm of political action the literary justice meted out in the earlier play. Here the state is in danger and demands action from its artists—the world has not yet been made safe for poetry.

The time of Cicero, of course, precedes that of Augustus, and we are presented with the chaos out of which the artist-statesman creates a new order, according to which future generations can and do (in *Poetaster)* regulate themselves.[19] Cicero's art, put to the service of truth and the state, re-creates Rome: "The common-wealth owes him a civicke gyrland./ He is the onely father of his countrey" *(C,* V.312–13). If he is the father—

19. That *Catiline* is in the chronology of Jonson's works later than *Poetaster* is immaterial in this regard. Jonson, having displayed aesthetic statecraft in flower, subsequently turned to show the ground from which it sprang.

and preserver—of Rome, he is, as Jonson must have been acutely aware, the preserver of Western civilization and humanistic tradition, of as much of the Truth as had been so far discovered by man. Since this was indeed the light in which Jonson always saw the artist, it is in his terms very fitting that the day on which such artistic honor and responsibility were successfully claimed should be forever celebrated:

> If those good dayes come no lesse gratefull to us,
> Wherein we are preserv'd from some great danger,
> Then those, wherein we'are borne, and brought to light,
> . . .
>   . . . why should not, then,
> This day, to us, and all posteritie
> Of ours, be had in equall fame, and honor,
> With that, when ROMULUS first rear'd these walls,
> When so much more is saved, then he built? (V.325–35)

Catiline contains the victory which is climax to both of Jonson's alternatives. The opponents are verbal artists *and* men of practical action, and both are men of action *through* their art. The identity of action and imagination also characterizes Mosca, Subtle, and, to some extent, Sejanus, but Jonson's treatments of this fusion were led up to by the series of plays in which the two possibilities—action plus art and action through art—are kept separate. We have seen action plus art in *Every Man in* (Clement) and *Poetaster* (Ovid, Augustus); action through art occupies *Every Man out* (Asper), *Cynthia's Revels* (Crites), and again *Poetaster* (Horace), the play in which these alternatives coexist for the first time and after which they become one. These three plays are Jonson's "Comicall satyres," and the guise of the socially effective artist is the role of the satirist.

"Before Ben Jonson's time the word *Satire* had not been applied to the drama"[20]—but Jonson added to the innovation of calling his plays poems the unprecedented claim that three of them (at least) were satires. The

20. Alexander Corbin Judson, ed., *Cynthia's Revels,* Yale Studies in English, 45 (New York, 1912), xxxii.

name "comicall satyre" indicated a combination of two genres whose close relationship had the sanction of Renaissance and classical critical tradition. Satire, the exposure of the follies and vices of individuals and society by means of "aggressive, censorious wit," was believed on the strength of Horace's assertion to hark back to the Old Comedy of the Greeks, from which Lucilius, the originator of Latin satire, drew his inspiration and model.[21] The Old Comedy, which culminated in the works of Aristophanes, had as its most outstanding characteristic a vigorous attack, frequently abusive, on contemporary manners and morals, and indeed on contemporaries. As a dramatic genre this satirical-abusive form had never become a part of English tradition. Comedy had evolved from the miracle and morality plays to take its place on the native stage, while verse satire, based first on the cheerful goliardic and Anglo-Norman writings, had under pressure of disintegrating religious and social conditions acquired "a fierce, mocking laughter" of its own, which "was doubtless the cause of the revival of interest in formal Latin satire."[22] But the two traditions, satiric and comic-dramatic, had remained separate. Jonson's decision to combine them was a deliberate affirmation of their affinities. He "was reasserting a relationship established when Lucilius and his Roman successors began to write and was re-establishing a type of comedy the

21. Oscar J. Campbell, *Comicall Satyre and Shakespeare's Troilus and Cressida* (San Marino, 1938), p. 6 and n. 13, quoting Quintus Horatius Flaccus, *Satires* 1.4.1–6. Horace's opinion on the origin of Roman satire was upheld by J. C. Scaliger, Heinsius, and Dacier, as well as later by Dryden, who, however, assigns the first dramatic Latin imitations of the Old Comedy to Livius Andronicus, a Grecian-born playwright who flourished considerably before Lucilius. He explains Horace's words to mean that Lucilius was the first *polished* author of Roman satire and close imitator of the Old Comedy. See John Dryden, "A Discourse concerning the Original and Progress of Satire," in W. P. Ker, ed., *Essays of John Dryden*, 2 (Oxford, 1900), 44–62.

22. G. R. Owst, *Literature and Pulpit in Medieval England* (Cambridge, England, 1933), p. 216, quoted in Alvin Kernan, *The Cankered Muse*, Yale Studies in English, 142 (New Haven, 1959), 40; and Campbell, *Comicall Satyre*, p. 24. For detailed discussion of the development of Renaissance English satire, see Campbell, Chap. 2; Kernan, Chap. 2; and C. R. Baskervill, *English Elements in Jonson's Early Comedy* (Austin, 1911), Chaps. 2 and 3.

aims and methods of which had once been accurately defined."[23] By his lights, he was reclaiming an island of Truth which was in danger of slipping out of sight of the shores of England.

Jonson was not the man to salvage land and materials without turning them to the use of his own building. The foundation of true insight which had been covered over, he excavated and displayed to the world: satire, the railing outbursts of a man at odds with his contemporaries, and comedy, the high-minded companion of tragedy, were sisters under the skin. This contention or, as Jonson would have preferred to call it, rediscovery enormously raised the dignity of English satire, which was now in the most exalted company, for "the parts of a Comedie are the same with a *Tragedie,* and the end is partly the same. For, they both delight, and teach: the *Comicks* are call'd διδάσκαλοι, of the *Greeks;* no lesse then the *Tragicks*" (D, 2625–28). These dicta were the cornerstones of Jonson's new structure, which had been laid by the ancients; but the design of the building was his own: "For I thanke those, that have taught me, and will ever: but yet dare not thinke the *scope* of their labour, and enquiry, was to envy their posterity, what they also could adde, and find out" (D, 146–49). Thus the induction to *Every Man out of His Humor,* Jonson's first Comicall Satyre, presents Cordatus, *"The Authors friend; A man inly acquainted with the scope and drift of his Plot: Of a discreet, and understanding judgement"* (description of Cordatus, 111–13), informing his fellow spectator Mitis that the play they are about to see is "strange, and of a particular kind by it selfe, somewhat like *Vetus Comoedia:* a worke that hath bounteously pleased me, how it will answere the generall expectation, I know not" (*"After the Second Sounding,"* 231–34).

Comicall Satyre is somewhat like the *Vetus Comoedia,* but it is not the same genre. Jonson was sufficiently involved in Renaissance theories of comedy to assimilate to his practice the ideals of the Greek New Comedy, which, "invariably regarded" by English critics of the sixteenth century "as the fountain-head of all Renaissance comedy, was distinguished from old comedy by its substitution of good-natured correction of faults

23. Baskervill, p. 7.

common to large numbers of men, for rough, impudent attacks on individuals."[24] Good-natured *Every Man out* is not; but for the rest its objectives correspond to this description of the New Comedy. For Jonson, who to all the observations of the Ancients applied his own experience that he might have the better means to pronounce *(D,* 134–37), did not pronounce entirely in favor of the *Vetus Comoedia.* With disapproval he noted that

> it was cleare that all insolent, and obscene speaches; jest[s] upon the best men; injuries to particular persons; perverse, and sinister Sayings (and the rather unexpected) in the old Comedy, did move laughter; especially, where it did imitate any dishonesty; and scurrility came forth in the place of wit. *(D,* 2646–51)

All these faults, and particularly the imitation of "any dishonesty"—which, considering the description, immediately following, of the slanders and impossible actions presented as true by the Old Comedy, I take to mean dishonest representation of an action or state of affairs—Jonson was most anxious to avoid. Each of his three Comicall Satyres portrays a poet engaged in the correction of his society; and for the Jonsonian poet, whose most basic object and duty was to "write things like the Truth" *(D,* 2353–54), the techniques of the Old Comedy were unthinkable.

They were not unthinkable, however, for the satirist. Indeed, in the native English satires and in those which relied on the Juvenalian tradition, they were standard procedure. Unembarrassed by his inconsistency, the satirist purports to stand apart from vice and folly in noble isolation, while at the same time brimming over with rage, bitterness, prurience, contempt, and a sense of personal injury amounting to paranoia. Clearly, only the first half of his personality could possibly correspond to that of Jonson's poet: the aspect which permitted the poet-satirist, like the poet-orator, to appear as a public figure closely related to or identical with the poet-statesman. But the traditional English satirist's private personality was such that he could not have been trusted with an assistant clerkship in the State Records Room, lest he scrawl obscene lampoons on his superi-

24. Campbell, *Satyre,* p. 12.

ors in the margins of his pages. This private personality was based partly on the native English tradition of the satirist as a rude, unlettered man of the lower classes; partly on the Elizabethan critical theory that the earliest origin of satire was the satyr play (preceding even the Old Comedy), in which individuals were scurrilously attacked by actors clothed as satyrs, "that were rude, lassivious and wanton of behavior";[25] and partly on the *saeva indignatio* of Juvenalian tradition, supposedly elicited by the frightful condition of the society in which the satirist was forced to live. As Kernan points out, the "justification of the 'squint-eyed sight' of the satyr" is "that it is necessary to employ a distorted lens to bring man's moral ugliness into true focus," and this justification "is not only stated in every satire of the period, but is latent in every aspect of the satyr's character" (not to be confused with the satirist's character). It is quite true that in the satiric tradition this private character of the satirist, all his "many moral weaknesses, his melancholy, his sadism, his prurience, his intemperance, are, paradoxically, the sources of his satiric strength."[26] Nonetheless, we find him in this guise boorish, vicious, intolerant and intolerable.

The traditional double character of the satirist presents openly and in an extreme form that doubleness of the imagination which Jonson perceived but refused to acknowledge. That part of the imagination which revels in the presentation of "moral ugliness," provided it takes arresting forms, which will even deliberately elicit or independently invent dramatic moral outrages in which potential evil may become actual, Jonson refused to see as an aspect of creativity. That it was a major aspect of his own creativity evidently stiffened—perhaps motivated—his rejection of it, while largely accounting for his fascination with it. This part of the imagination is what operates in his perverse artists: an unfettered pleasure in "the follies"—and crimes—"of their flesh" (P, IV.9.109). Once he had recognized it, Jonson took care always to banish it to the mind of an "unworthy" character, so that it might operate contained by the sanction of the author's moral disapproval and might satisfy itself without

25. Thomas Langley, *An Abridgemente of the Notable Works of Polidore Vergile* (1570), sigs. cii–ciii, quoted in Kernan, *Muse,* p. 55.

26. Kernan, p. 136.

bringing moral suspicion upon its creator. Brainworm is its first—very weak—representative, and here Jonson does not see his own implications. Clement first chastens Brainworm but then elevates him into a kind of hero, a confusion of moral judgment which muddles the play. Here is a pull between two incompatible standards: private amoral entertainment and social utility. In his next play *(EO)*, Jonson tries to reconcile these by making the former the secular arm of the latter; in the following play *(CR)*, he represses nonmoral imagination altogether; then he comes upon the idea of the scapegoat and achieves the pure Horace and Virgil at the cost of the tainted Ovid—a turning point in his work, as we have seen, because he acknowledges for the first time the immoral, destructive *artist*. Fascination with the successes of this new character meant the end of "comicall satyre," based as it was on the assumption that what succeeds is good-poetry-as-action, until finally confrontation between that part of imagination Jonson was prepared to allow and that part which was under a taboo produced the tragical satire of *Catiline*.

The clearest presentation of this doubleness of imagination, the analogous traditional doubleness of the satirist, and Jonson's peculiar position in denying that it forms one harmonious whole comes in *Every Man out*, where Jonson solves his problem with the wisdom of Solomon: he divides the satirist in half. To the half named Asper he assigns the public, or Horatian, satirical character; to the half named Macilente, the private, or Juvenalian, character. Asper, the "author" of the play to be presented, represents the kind of poet who writes "comicall satyre"; Jonson saw himself as an individual specimen of the genus Asper. To Asper belongs the frank, open, indignant attitude of the good man who is capable of being the good poet. It is not quite accurate to say that he is entirely Horatian, since the asperity he derives from his name and function passes beyond the bounds of the suavely conversational tone of the Roman poet, and he sees the society he attacks as not only foolish but depraved. It is in his own character that he resembles Horace—in his freedom from the vices he attacks and in his courage, untainted by self-seeking, to attack them in the face of his enemies' hatred and the warnings of his friends. Jonson has endowed him with the forceful language and typical imagery of the satyr-satirist, but has reserved the normally concomitant moral blemishes to Macilente, into whom Asper turns himself for the purpose of taking part in the play itself, to purge its extravagant characters of their humors.

Asper's seriousness of moral purpose is a foretaste of Cicero's. His description of "this impious world" foreshadows *Catiline's* Rome:

> the earth, crackt with the weight of sinne,
> Helle gaping under us, and o're our heads
> Blacke rav'nous ruine, with her saile-stretcht wings,
> Ready to sink us downe, and cover us.
>
> *(EO, "After the Second Sounding," 8–11)*

Like Caesar and the conspirators, Asper's contemporaries have been told of the afterlife assigned to the wicked, but scoff at religion and continue in their vicious courses:

> And yet not one of these but knowes his workes,
> Knowes what damnation is, the devill, and hell,
> Yet, hourely they persist, grow ranke in sinne,
> Puffing their soules away in perj'rous aire,
> To cherish their extortion, pride, or lusts.
>
> *("After the Second Sounding," 32–36)*

Under these fearful circumstances, Asper, like Cicero, must speak. He cannot "behold such prodigies as these,/ And have his lips seal'd up"; he feels the necessity of action, and

> (with an armed, and resolved hand)
> Ile strip the ragged follies of the time,
> Naked, as at their birth: . . .
>   . . . and with a whip of steele,
> Print wounding lashes in their yron ribs.
>
> *("After the Second Sounding," 12–13, 16–20)*

Like Cicero and every true poet, Asper has had his education with the gods; it is the loss of the divine pattern that causes his mental and moral anguish. The typical satirist, "Timon-like, appears to hate the world now and scourge it because he once loved it and was disappointed by it."[27] This is exactly the position of Asper and, eventually, of the embittered Jonson himself. It is in fact the inescapable position, finally, of the satirist who derives his justification not merely from his didactic powers, which may have some chance of success, but from his special vision of the divine plan. He is caught, by the very nature of his calling, in the hapless situation of Peacock's Rosicrucian, "who will love nothing but a sylph, who does not believe in the existence of a sylph, and who yet quarrels with the whole universe for not containing a sylph."[28] All false sylphs, all frivolous women, all follies and all crimes are but symptoms of the world's decay, to which Jonson refers again and again as an accepted fact in the *Discoveries*. The poet-satirist is actually dealing not with the reformation of manners but with the presentation of a postlapsarian world, which he opposes, in his mind and in the mind of his audience, to the prelapsarian world unknowable to man as he now is, knowable only to the poet in his moments of semi-madness. Though what man sees through art may change and correct him, it can never do so to the satisfaction of the artist who has seen the vision in its undistorted glory. Cordatus perceives all this very well when he tells Asper:

> Unlesse your breath had power
> To melt the world, and mould it new againe,
> It is in vaine, to spend it in these moods.
>
> *("After the Second Sounding,"* 48–50)

"To melt the world, and mould it new againe" is precisely the power Jonson finally gives to Cicero, enabling the satirist to act against, not with, the malicious enjoyment of immorality. But Asper's nobility is still depen- dent upon the activities of Macilente, eminently successful in his attempt to shock his fellow characters out of their humors with his various tricks and intrigues, most of them quite as distasteful as the original humors. It is he who uses the methods of the *Vetus Comoedia*. His overwhelming motivation is envy; he is a man who, "(wanting that place in the worlds

27. Ibid., p. 110.
28. Thomas Love Peacock, *Nightmare Abbey* (London, Hamish Hamil- ton, 1947), p. 70.

account, which he thinks his merit capable of) falls into such an envious apoplexie, with which his judgement is so dazeled, and distasted, that he growes violently impatient of any opposite happinesse in another" *(EO,* description of Macilente, 9–13). Out of this impatience grows his opposition to the other characters; there is no selfless indignation in him. Cordatus makes the distinction when he explains why Macilente hates the rich miser Sordido:

> you must understand, Signior, he envies him not as he is a villaine, a wolfe i' the common-wealth, but as he is rich, and fortunate; for the true condition of envie is, *Dolor alienae foelicitatis* ... Whereas, if we make his monstrous, and abhord actions our object, the griefe (we take then) comes neerer the nature of hate, then envie. (I.3.162–70)

Macilente is not only envious, mean-spirited, and generally destructive; his attractive emotional makeup includes lust for his host's wife and sadism gratified by the poisoning of Puntarvolo's little dog as part of the successful scheme to rid that knight of his humor.

In all this he is doing no more than the traditional satirist is entitled to do. Even his motivation is acceptable:

> In believing envy to be the emotion most competent to effect the exposure and derision of human folly, Jonson is adopting a psychological theory at least as old as Plato ... the idea that envy is that mixed feeling of pain and pleasure which opens a critic's eye to ridiculous aspects of human conduct and sharpens his pen when displaying them.[29]

But the crucial point is that Macilente has no pen. He is not fit to wield it. Asper holds the pen, Macilente the vial of poison. The locus of relationships between Macilente and the humor characters is a circle concentric with that larger one formed by Asper's relationship to the audience. Each of these is strictly determined: Asper cannot step in and Macilente cannot step out. Asper attacks vice by writing his play; his honesty enables him to do this effectively. To scourge the fools within the play, he employs the further creation of his mind, Macilente. He is what Jonson, possessed

29. Campbell, *Satyre,* p. 59.

by his concept of the incorruptible poet, regarded as the uncreative half of the traditional satirist; he represents only a powerful (if meanly motivated) agent of correction, not any form of satiric author. In formal verse-satire and critical discussions of the genre the satyr-satirist is set forth as writer of the works in question; but Macilente does not write. The very qualities which make him effective as satyr-satirist would, for Jonson, disable him from being a poet-satirist.

In this conjunction of the poet-satirist with the satyr-satirist may be seen the typical linking by the formal satirists of Truth and Envy as presiding deities for their verses:

> Envy wayts on my backe, Truth on my side:
> Envy will be my Page, and Truth my Guide.
> Envy the margent holds, and Truth the line:
> Truth doth approve, but Envy doth repine.[30]

But Jonson's different, purely moralistic division of labor between Truth and Envy is the beginning of the satyr's ostracism from the company of decent creators. Even at the end of *Every Man out,* immoral imagination is annihilated—Macilente is retransformed into Asper, on the pretext that immorality is only a means to morality: "I am . . . emptie of all envie now" (V.11.55), Macilente announces before vanishing. By the time of *Poetaster* such a transformation can no longer take place; the roles of Macilente and Asper have been definitively differentiated from one another, as is clear from the first reasoned apologia assigned not to the satirist himself but to an exalted champion:

> His [Horace's] sharpenesse, that is most excusable;
> As being forc't out of a suffering vertue
> Oppressed with the licence of the time.
> 'Tis not the wholesome sharp moralitie
> Or modest anger of a *satyricke* spirit,
> That hurts, or wounds the bodie of a state;
> But the sinister application

---

30. Joseph Hall, *Virgidemiarum,* Lib. I, Prologue, Sig. B, quoted in Campbell, p. 60.

Of the malicious, ignorant, and base
Interpreter: who will distort, and straine
The generall scope and purpose of an authour,
To his particular, and private spleene. *(P,* V.3.368–70, 138–44)

Besides this conveniently anonymous "interpreter," Ovid stands by to
assume the burden of fleshly weakness as it drops from Horace's chaste
shoulders. Indeed, except for the general discomfort Horace may (or may
not) experience because of the poetic abuses around him, it is hard to see
how his virtue is "suffering." It seems to flourish, fertilized by an amount
of appreciation, understanding, and unlimited trust seldom accorded that
fair plant, and illuminated by the sunshine of public favor.

Between these two plays falls *Cynthia's Revels,* an interesting whitewash
job. Here Crites, "Whom PHOEBUS (though not Fortune) holdeth
deare" (V.6.92), is indeed the perfect sufferer. With no Macilente to
relieve his mental agony and no Ovid to show up his poetical virtue
for the populace, he must get along as best he can with divine revelation.
In this play Jonson denies, with disastrous dramatic results, any conflict
between the moral and immoral halves of artistry. The only conflict is
between the divine and the mundane—that simplistic conflict talked
about, though not exhibited, in *Every Man in.* Here it is exhibited; here
Jonson presents his ideal poet in an ideally obtuse society, without complexity, without qualification, without antithesis, and without reality.
What has been dimly foreshadowed by Knowell Junior and inculcated by
negative precept through Ovid, what has taken historical form in Horace
and Cicero and split off, in Asper, from Macilente, now presents one
allegorical whole in Crites.

Crites' very unreality enables him to be a perfect incarnation of the
theoretical poet alluded to in *Discoveries.* The very simplicity which
makes him dramatically a failure and a bore assures his conceptual usefulness and interest. Here, with a clarity and firmness made possible by
deliberate repression of undesired knowledge, Jonson sums up exactly
the poet he has in mind. Here is the morally flawless being, aligned with
the forces of nature: "One, in whom the humours and elements are
peaceably met, without emulation of precedencie . . . but in all, so

composde & order'd, as it is cleare, *Nature* went about some ful worke, she did more then make a man, when she made him" (II.4.124–30). He is natural yet more than natural, a created creator, composed "not of usuall earth,/ But of that nobler, and more precious mould,/ Which PHOEBUS selfe doth temper" (V.8.22–24). Like the physician, whose inspiration also comes from Apollo, he wishes not to destroy but to make whole:

> What wise physician have we ever seene
> Moov'd with a frantike man? the same affects
> That he doth beare to his sicke patient,
> Should a right mind carry to such as these.[31] *(CR, III.3.33–36)*

The holy trinity to which his "right mind" turns for aid is composed of inspiration ("PHOEBUS APOLLO: . . . with ancient rites,/ And due devotions, I have ever hung/ Elaborate *paeans*, on thy golden shrine"), of invention *("Cyllenian* MERCURY (sweet MAIAS joy)/ . . . in the busie tumults of the mind,/ My path thou ever hast illumined"), and of virtue ("O thou, the very power, by which I am,/ . . ./Admired ARETE (of them admir'd,/ Whose soules are not enkindled by the sense)/ Disdaine not my chaste fire")—all servants, but also all aspects, of the heavenly Cynthia (V.5.59–61, 65–67, 49–54).

This Allegoricall Satyre is really a dramatized essay on the nature of satire. Its semi-mythical characters free it from the shadows of personal animosity at the same time that Crites, by inventing and producing a socially corrective play within a play, assimilates to the role of Asper that of Macilente, but in the true manner of a poet. His play is a masque of the eternal verities, in which each of the misbehaving courtiers plays the virtue opposed to his vice. That is, Crites fayneth and formeth a fable,

31. Here Crites agrees with Asper, who wishes to show "the times deformitie/ Anatomiz'd in every nerve, and sinnew" and offers to his audience "phisicke of the mind" *("After the Second Sounding,"* 120–21, 132), as well as with Horace, who actually administers the bitter pill, and with Jonson himself: "If men may by no meanes write freely, or speake truth, but when it offends not; why doe *Physicians* cure with sharp medicines, or corrosives? Is not the same equally lawfull in the cure of the minde, that is in the cure of the body?" *(D, 2313–17).*

and writes things like the Truth (D, 2353–54); this re-creation of Truth
is the essence of satire.

In accordance with his divine vision, Crites himself strives toward
the divine,[32] and the object of his work is to form society and his fellowman to the divine pattern, the eternal object of the poet-satirist:

> That, these vaine joyes, in which their wills consume
> Such powers of wit, and soule, as are of force
> To raise their beings to aeternitie,
> May be converted on . . .
> . . .
> . . . the native frame of a true heart,
> An inward comeliness of bountie, knowledge,
> And spirit, that may conforme them, actually,
> To *Gods* high figures, which they have in power:
> Which to neglect for a selfe-loving neatnesse,
> Is sacrilege, of an unpardon'd greatnesse. (V.4.637–48)

At the end of the play Crites becomes what Jonson believed the
satirist essentially to be: the representative of divine justice, public
justice, and poetic justice—the defender of reality against false appearance, who orders the miscreants to bathe themselves in the well of
knowledge, until, "purged of your present maladies,/ (Which are not
few, nor slender) you become/ Such as you faine would seeme"
(V.11.154–56). He has assumed his proper role as public poet and
public man, yet he remains also what he was before, a man apart—not
only socially, in a society too corrupt to appreciate him, but through
intellectual (and scholarly) pre-eminence and through his gifts as a
Seer. Though he undertakes the combined functions of judge and ruler
and becomes a man of action through his art, though his artistic action
accomplishes its purpose and does communicate some part of his vision,
he remains removed from the world of flux, standing apart from the

---

32. V.10.97–105. When Cupid asks Mercury why the arrows of sensual
love cannot pierce Crites, Mercury replies that as Cynthia and her attendants
are impervious to Cupid's power because they are divine, so Crites is impervious because he aspires to be divine.

satiric scene as the physician stands apart from his patient. Sympathy he must possess; empathy he dare not. Despite his love of beauty, he abjures the physical side of life except insofar as it is a necessity, creating in himself a perfect balance between the aesthetic and the ascetic. He is not ashamed to be looked down upon or afraid to forgo worldly advantages for his art, but neither is he so humble as to be afraid, or ashamed, to censure moral ugliness.

Because Asper, Crites, and Horace corresponded in their satirical function to Jonson himself, contemporaries and subsequent critics took him to task, with more or less ridicule and disapproval, for having presumed to declare implicitly that he himself was this perfect synthesis of "a most ingenuous and sweet spirit, a sharp and season'd wit, a straight judgment, and a strong mind" *(CR,* II.3.137–39). But this is to confuse aspiration with conceit. What is troubling is Jonson's stubborn belief that such a paragon could exist and should exist, that he ought to be made to exist by denying or banishing all his "base" impulses, and that such purity was a desirable goal for Jonson himself. But the poet as presented in this chapter was for Jonson the ideal poet; though Jonson felt himself fitted by nature, inclination, and industry to strive toward the ideal, he did not assert that he had attained it. The charges of his detractors are valid only insofar as Jonson did consider himself a man of the same species as that of which Asper, Crites, and Horace were outstanding examples. He felt his goals to be the same as theirs: the construction of a model universe, on a tiny scale, which would correspond to the real universe of eternal truth and would at once shame and inspire its beholders. When it failed to do so, he was horrified and enraged, not merely because he felt himself denied the applause which was his due, but because he was dismayed and indignant at the inability of his fellowmen to perceive truth, though made plain by the best efforts of art. When, for their better understanding, he set himself to "strip the ragged follies of the time,/ Naked, as at their birth" *(EO, "After the Second Sounding,"* 17–18), he saw his audience "blush for anger, not for shame,/ And turn shewn nakednesse to impudence" *(CR,* V.4.627–28).

His struggle was not only with his audience; it was also with his art. He felt strongly that poetry must suit the times, for how else could it communicate moral insight to the mass of men? But to suit the times was difficult, almost impossible, without compromising the moral insight itself. His lifelong problem was not merely a clash of erudition with desire for popularity; it was the problem of transforming the base matter of the world into a spiritual elixir, the age-old problem of the philosopher.

That Jonson called his ideal poet not Poeta but Crites (originally Criticus) suggests Jonson's way to a solution of the problem: to apply to every fragment of his art not only the creative imagination but the critical intelligence, to ask not only, Is it inspired? but, Is it correct?— that is, well rendered and, above all, true. This tendency in him not only to portray but to judge has brought him his greatest praise and his greatest condemnation. "He was in English drama the great censurer who brought . . . a critical sense of life to his imaginative art as no one else has done," the critic acclaims him; but only to add immediately, "Usually he wrote too much from the intellect, and too little from the heart."[33] This is a strangely uncomprehending criticism to level against a man engaged in applying all the force of his mind, all the synthesizing powers of his intellect, to reveal a moral order in apparent chaos. It might be better to look for understanding to the philosopher, with whom Jonson as poet has his obstacles and his triumphs in common:

> It is a romantic fallacy—the fallacy of pure art and of pure inspira-
> tion—that creative imagination and abstract, philosophical thought
> are naturally opposed faculties of the mind, the one necessarily in-
> hibiting the other. Rather there is an impression of shallowness and
> flimsiness, of a dimension missing, in the work of poets who had
> evidently not thought deeply about their own aesthetic principles
> and about the relation of art to morality.[34]

33. Rhys, *Ben Jonson*, pp. 26, 25.
34. Stuart Hampshire, "An Act of Resignation" (review of T. S. Eliot's *On Poetry and Poets*), *Encounter*, 10, No. 1 (1958), 73.

2. First Appearances

It is only shallow people who do not judge by appearances.

Oscar Wilde, The Picture of Dorian Gray, Chap. 2

When Jonson set himself to explore and exploit, to the utmost of his capacity, "the relation of art to morality," he assumed the poet's and prophet's burden of conveying the Truth. But the prophet, by tradition, is an unpopular man with an unacceptable message, while the poet, according to Jonson, makes the truth apparent and inescapable for the men to whom he speaks. It will not suffice for him to exclaim with the prophet that his message is plain and unavoidable; if he wishes to be believed, he, like the prophet, must provide a visible sign which cannot be denied. Though "Truth is mans proper good; and the onely *immortall* thing, was given our mortality to use. No good *Christian,* or *Ethnick,* if he be honest, can misse it" (D, 531–33), yet Truth is (likening great things to small) as a side road: an affirmation that you cannot miss it is sufficient assurance that you will. The network of roads is too large for the eye to encompass, words too unlike roads to be dependable guides. What is wanted is not description but demonstration—a paradigm, a picture, a map. Jonson was too adept at communication not to perceive that every message must have its bottle if it is to come to land. The relation of his plays to absolute Truth is the relation of a map to the countryside: the artifact contains not "truths, but things (like truths) well fain'd" *(SW,* Second Prologue, 10).

Truth, for Jonson, takes two forms: practical and metaphysical. Practical truth consists in what is or has been actually the case. "Things like" practical truth are either reconstructions of actual events or inventions of such as could have happened. The first conform to historical, the second to naturalistic, truth—both aspects of the practical. This goes some way toward explaining the apparent paradox critics have found in Jonson's work: that a man on the one hand so attentive to "realistic" detail should on the other have devoted such scrupulous care to historical accuracy that in plays which demand the latter it quite outweighs the former and very nearly sinks the work. "Realism" and supposed pedantry, far from waging a battle to the death in his tormented soul, marched side by side under the banner of practical truth.

The criteria of what could have happened are not only practical, however. Jonson's view of the ideal poet rested squarely on the assumption that there is a stable order regulating all events which constitutes metaphysical Truth and which can, because of its stability and earthly effectiveness, be demonstrated and imitated by the poet as well as comprehended by his audience. Thus his manner of constructing his plays derives from his belief in the ideal poet's task—or, more precisely, both his theory about poets and his dramatic practice derive from the same belief in a stable metaphysical Truth. The question is, what did Jonson think this Truth was? The construction of his plays contains the answer. To trace the implications of the overall patterns which recur in all Jonson's plays, regardless of individual plot, is to outline his picture of a stable universe and the principles on which it is ordered.

The Truthful Pattern

Jonson's plots are concerned with three principal themes: the discovery of real relationships, the curing of wrongheadedness, and the exposure of chicanery. From the romantic long-lost brother contrivances of *The Case Is Altered* to the intrigues of the disguised witch in *The Sad*

Shepherd, every play Jonson ever wrote revolves around some combination of these three central issues. The plots play variations on his principal theme, endless inversions of the same leitmotiv, which signals approaching revelation. There are certain actions the universe itself will not permit: *"No lye ever growes old"* (D, 542). The universe is truthful. Further, "no ill can happen to a *good* man. Contraries are not mixed" *(D, 9–10)*. The universe is just; the universe is consistent. Nature, the administrator on earth of this divine impulse toward truth, directs earthly affairs in such a way that nothing determined by her presents an appearance that does not correspond to its reality; furthermore, she brings to light any attempted deceit. "Things like" metaphysical truth are invented actions which illustrate these principles, and the plot of every one of Jonson's plays is an exemplum for the text, "Nothing is lasting that is fain'd; it will have another face then it had, ere long" *(D, 540–42)*.

The pattern is always the same. The protagonists are about to make a more or less serious mistake, the consequences of which they suffer or (less often) discover in the nick of time.[1] They have in common their uncommon gullibility, for their mistakes are traceable to one source: they misinterpret the universe in which they live. Either the truth is disguised from them or they disguise it from themselves by wrongheadedness. In both cases they are disabled, willingly or not, from working with Nature, and it is the task of the play to correct their cosmic invalidism.

1. To take one example from each play, a character may: entrust a chaste sweetheart to the care of a libidinous friend *(CA)*, think a true wife false or a false wife true *(EI, EO)*, undertake the role of a virtue while possessing the attributes of a vice *(CR)*, institute blasphemous revels which lead to banishment *(P)*, overingratiate himself with an emperor whose favor is thus lost *(S)*, take a miserly misanthrope on the point of lechery for a generous benefactor on the point of death *(V)*, deliver all his worldly goods to be turned into gold *(A)*, overestimate his conspiratorial abilities and his confederates' honesty *(C)*, place his trust in criminals *(BF)*, marry a boy in place of a woman *(SW)*, lose his estate to schemers *(DA)*, fail to recognize a sister disguised as a brother *(NI)*, squander his patrimony under observation by a supposedly dead father *(SN)*, accept wanton maid as chaste mistress and vice versa *(ML)*, raise the hue and cry over a nonexistent highway robbery *(TT)*, or quarrel with a witch in the shape of a mistress *(SS)*.

The turn of events invariably puts cure within the reach of society, over which the healthful sunshine of reality plays when the facts emerge. That in some works *(BF, S, A)* individual men or entire societies are better content with darkness visible makes these pieces not exceptions to the basic structure that causes truth to be revealed but rather modifications of what otherwise appears to be an optimistic view of man's potentialities.

Metaphysical truth is thus illustrated by the pattern of the play as a whole, and practical truth by the specific actions within it. What does happen must be regulated by what can happen; the sum of everything that does happen, in the closed world of art, is what can happen. The sum of all the practical truth in a drama by Jonson is the metaphysical truth that Nature aligns appearance with reality, and the corollary that any misalignment must be the fault of man.

Since the poet is the instrument of perfect alignment, Jonson had a double purpose in the creation of his dramatic world. One half was the inculcation of metaphysical truth through the metaphysical principles upon which his plays were constructed and through accurate imitation of that practical truth which contains the metaphysical. The second, too often taken for the whole, was to make practical correction in the lives of men, in order to lead them to metaphysical harmony with a moral universe. This second task Jonson performed with such excellence that critics, peering into the mirror his plays held up to Nature, have tended to see nothing but unlovely human faces and to write the experience off as another encounter—perhaps more startling than most—with the didactic satire of the age. The concept that poetry teaches by positive and negative precept is indeed, as we have seen, strongly operative in Jonson's work and in his statements about it; but "Jonson's didactic theory is more philosophical than moral, more literary than monitory."[2] He did wish to reform patterns of behavior, but he wished primarily to show a world behaving in patterns: he was more concerned with exposition than exposure.

2. Helena Watts Baum, *The Satiric and the Didactic in Ben Jonson's Comedy* (Chapel Hill, 1947), pp. 22–23.

The stage presented an opportunity equaled by no other show place of poetry for construction of both the metaphysical and practical scaffolding of Jonson's universe. Neither in the epic nor in any form of the lyric, not even in formal satire, could the poet command the conviction elicited by living people speaking and acting under the beholders' very eyes. Only on the stage is there full scope for the illusion that what is presented *must* be true, since it happens while the audience watches. When Asper, employing the traditional imagery of the satirist, offers to oppose to his spectators' eyes "a mirror,/ As large as is the stage whereon we act" *(EO, "After the Second Sounding,"* 118–19), he can promise himself and them not only a metaphorical but also a physical surface upon which will in fact appear images of men moving according to the laws of Nature. Since the poet is to the play as Nature is to the world, if he makes the laws of his creation the same which he has perceived in the universe, his little world will be a sure guide to the greater—provided he can get his audience to accept it. In part, the visible microcosm of the stage serves that function: it renders the poet's conceptual microcosm persuasive. The solid boards reinforce a poetic concept of the workings of the universe.

The Truthful Name

Jonson's distinctive poetic concept, the fusion of practical and metaphysical truth in the framework of his plays, is nowhere more striking than in the principles of his naming. "The custom of naming a character to reflect his personality was common, but the persistent practice of punning on the name seems to have been more common with Jonson,"[3] remarks one of his editors with restraint. In fact, Jonson carried his search for and insistence upon such puns to lengths unimagined and undesired by any contemporary poet, causing a modern specialist on the subject to ask but never answer the question: "how did it happen that Jonson, diverging from most of his contemporaries, placed

3. William Edward Selin, ed., *The Case Is Altered,* Yale Studies in English, 56 (New Haven, 1917), p. xxiii.

so much value on the correspondence between name and bearer?"[4] "Contraries are not mixed," and Jonson, assuming the role of Nature, gave to each man the name that described his essence. But to demonstrate the eternal coincidence of appearance and reality, the impossibility of lasting deceit, he permitted himself to be a little less obscure than Nature. Everyday names are suggestive; one can feel that an acquaintance is or is not correctly named. But it is easier to discern the essence marked "Fitz-Dottrell" or "Peniboy" than that labeled "Robert" or "Michael." Jonson erects a subjective effect into an objective one, implying that there are indeed essential qualities in names which can be intuitively perceived.

This belief comes out plainly even in the early *The Case Is Altered*, in which his naming technique has not yet fully crystallized. While here he assigns openly allusive names only to minor characters, a practice more usual in his age than was his later custom, major characters are given names acceptable as real. He has not yet gone sufficiently far from truths toward "things like" truths to apply his subsequent technique, in which the existence in his plays of essence-names stands for the existence in the real world of common names with essences. In *The Case Is Altered* he attempts the more difficult task of selecting for at least some of his major characters genuine names factually associated with the qualities outstanding in his characters. Thus Chamount, a French soldier, is probably named for a French general Chaumont, and Maximilian, a general of the Milanese, for the German Emperor Maximilian Pate, who in 1508 conquered the city of Vicenza.[5] (The latter supposition is encouraged by the German form of the name, occurring, contrary to Jonson's custom, in a play set in Italy.) If Maximilian was a great conqueror in Italy, then "Maximilian" must mean "great conqueror in Italy"; that one particular

4. Otto Hinze, *Studien zu Ben Jonsons Namengebung in seinen Dramen* (Leipzig, 1919), p. 28: "wie kam es, dass Jonson abweichend von den meisten seiner Zeitgenossen so viel Wert auf die Uebereinstimmung von Namen und Träger legte?"

5. Ibid., p. 17. The form Chamount derives from the orthographic interchange of "a" and "au" before nasals and the anglicization of "mont" to "mount," both frequent in Elizabethan spelling.

Maximilian was a German emperor is a minor point, an element extraneous to what Jonson fixed upon as the name's essence. If Chaumont is the name of a noble French soldier, then for Jonson's purposes it becomes equivalent to "noble French soldier," and when he puts a noble French soldier in a play, he names him Chamount.

This tendency is still visible as late as *The Alchemist,* in two names which, contrary to what investigation has shown to be Jonson's nearly invariable practice,[6] do not correspond to the English setting: Ananias and Pertinax. Ananias, the Puritan whose zeal is greatest for immediate monetary gain, is the namesake of "the varlet/ That cozen'd the apostles" *(A,* II.5.72–73) by withholding from his contribution to them part of the price he had received for his land (Acts 5:1–5). His opposite, Pertinax Surly, the honest man whose honesty brings him only misfortune, is probably the godchild of a Roman emperor of whom Dion's history reports: "Pertinax lost his life in the attempt to better evil conditions in a brief space of time."[7] Jonson's knowledge of relatively obscure historical sources seems to have been inexhaustible; his use of these to provide fitting names for his creatures testifies to his perfectionism in aligning inner and outer qualities, for some of his choices must have been unknown to all but one or two auditors, and their outer appearance can have given inner satisfaction only to the author.

> Indeed, there is a woundy luck in names, Sirs
> And a maine mysterie, an' a man knew where
> To vind it. *(TT,* "The *Scene* interloping" [after IV.1], 1–3)

The luck and the mystery are that names exactly characterize their bearers. In the whole range of Jonson's dramas, including even the historical

6. Ibid., p. 27.

7. Dion, *Roman History* 37.10.3, quoted in Hinze, p. 36. Hinze's discussion of the name is on pp. 35–36, where he explains the unlikelihood of the name's being the Latin adjective by pointing to Jonson's consistent avoidance of language differences between name and environment, except when the name is an existing proper name in another language. It may be added in support of Hinze's opinion that Surly is no more pertinacious than the characters around him.

tragedies, 65 percent of all names allude to qualities in the bearer—
rather than to his profession or place of birth, for instance—and these
qualities are mainly spiritual.[8] Even apparent exceptions, in major
characters, turn out to be only increased subtleties reflecting upon the
theme of the play as a whole.

Such a name may, for instance, call attention to a delicate distinction.
Neither Sir Dauphine Eugenie nor Sir Amorous La-Foole is a French-
man, but the justification for the two names is very different. Sir Amorous
La-Foole's name declares him a combination of English and French; indeed, he says he is descended from the *"french* LA-FOOLES" *(SW,*
I.4.41), though related to those of England: "They all come out of our
house, the LA-FOOLES o' the north, the LA-FOOLES of the west, the
LA-FOOLES of the east, and south—we are as ancient a family, as any
is in *Europe" (SW,* I.4.37–40). He is a particular sort of fool: a Frenchified
Englishman, no solid stock about him, showing, beside the heavy oak
stubbornness of Morose (a fool in his own dour way), as no more than
plywood overlaid with lacquer. So pliant is he that he belongs to either
and neither sex. He is nominally masculine, or rather half-nominally, for
he is Sir Amorous; but he is also La-Foole, feminine in article and
ending, effeminate in dress and mannerism, boasting of feminine conquests of which he is incapable (his effeminacy is underscored by the
revelation that one of his "conquests" is actually a boy). This doubly
edged, or rather doubly blunt, name ties in with the play's main symbol
of enfeebled morality: the spiritual or theoretical hermaphrodite, as represented also by the masculine ladies of the Academy and most perfectly by the figure who provides the play's revealing title, Epicoene
her(him)self.

Sir Dauphine, on the other hand, has about him the better qualities
traditionally ascribed to the French: courtliness, delicacy, polish. His
name is consistent: he is not trying to harmonize artificial French effete-
ness with a heavy-handed English inner man. His courtliness is substantiated by his given name, which suggests not only princely deportment but also his position as Morose's rightful heir. There is a stab of

8. Hinze, p. 29.

psychological penetration reminiscent of Spenser in making Eugenie, incarnation of naturally refined good spirits (εὐγένιος, well-born; εὐ+ génie, good spirit),[9] the nearest relative of Morose, and his heir once he becomes tractable.

Repeatedly, apparent inconsistency in naming thus reveals itself as meticulous distinction. Knowell Junior and his friend Wellbred (EI) are youthful scapegraces, but their spirits are no higher than they are deep. Knowell is committed throughout to his knowledge of the value of poetry, while Wellbred's basic character, from which he has only temporarily departed, is delineated earlier by his brother:

Me thought he bare himselfe in such a fashion,
So full of man, and sweetnesse in his carriage,
And (what was chiefe) it shew'd not borrowed in him,
But all he did, became him as his owne,
And seem'd as perfect, proper, and possest
As breath, with life, or colour, with the bloud. (EI, Folio, II.1.47–52)

Essentially he is a man truly well bred; Jonson does not say that a good man cannot make mistakes. This natural breeding, along with good humor and understanding of both spiritual values (Known Well by Knowell Junior) and practical values (Known Well by Knowell Senior), underlies the balanced and creative society Justice Clement advocates at the end of the play.

The metaphysical truth here adumbrated is not merely that a name fits its bearer but that intention is more important than action. "It is the mind, and not the event, that distinguisheth the courtesie from wrong" (D, 462–63). To be essentially on the right side is sufficient warrant for bearing a positive name. Truewit's stratagems may not all be either truly witty or truly helpful, but he is on the right side, directing his wit to the proper goals, attempting to assist Sir Dauphine Eugenie in assisting Nature against his unnatural uncle. In his judgment of men Jonson was both harsher and more merciful than Aristotle, who declared that "life consists in action, and its end is a mode of action, not a

9. Ibid., p. 43.

quality. Now character determines men's qualities, but it is by their actions that they are happy or the reverse."[10] Jonson seems rather to have considered the end of life, in a society ideally constructed, a state of being. His perfectly virtuous characters all seem to act only when called upon, in case of necessity; the less perfectly virtuous engage in action while their natures and their society are in a state of flux. The ideal end is the attainment of a harmony close to stillness. Jonson is harsher than Aristotle because in his plays no man can be happy by means of his actions if he is not a good character; he is more merciful because no man can be the reverse if his character is good: "no ill can happen to a *good* man."

Not only the truthfulness of Nature but the skill of the poet is involved in Jonson's adherence to the principle that the name and the essential thing are one. If each created thing has an essence whereby it can be named, the poet's ability to name correctly is, like Adam's, proof of his insight, making of the poet not only a truthful but a true artist. Accordingly, none but the very earliest plays contain exceptions, in characters even relatively major, to the rules of essence-naming. Apart from these, the only departures (nearly all in the last comedies) are a character here and there so minor as to be insignificant.

At the height of his power Jonson's belief in the name as a semi-mystical sign of essence and destiny seems to have been absolute. For reasons already partially discussed, it is to be expected that his naming in *Poetaster* and the two Roman tragedies (as also in the historical fragment *Mortimer*) should correspond "almost slavishly"[11] to that in his sources. Since the personages of the play had existed, it was imperative that their real names, which represented their real essences, be preserved. To assign actual events to persons other than those who had brought them about, to assign them perhaps to persons whose names indicated a different motivation and destiny from those Nature had assigned, would be unforgivable misrepresentation. Insofar as men are the authors of events, inattention to names would mean depicting an event as springing

---

10. Aristotle, *Poetics*, 1450a 17–19, in S. H. Butcher, *Aristotle's Theory of Poetry and Fine Art* (4th ed. London, 1927), p. 27.

11. Hinze, *Ben Jonsons Namengebung*, p. 18.

from causes other than those which had actually effected it. These causes Jonson, being an artist rather than a reporter, wished in part to interpret. Relying on his poetic insight, he undertook to explain within his plays the hitherto unexplained significance of certain historical names, demonstrating for his audience, by citing actual examples, that the streams of practical truth flow to the ocean of metaphysics.

Fulvia, Curius, Lentulus, and Bestia appear in Sallust's account of Catiline's conspiracy; but for Jonson this account was only the raw material to be shaped (though without violation of the shape divinely intended for it) by the interpretation of art.[12] Although "of Fulvia nothing more is known than Sallust's statement that she was of noble birth,"[13] Jonson knew more: her name is a feminine variant of *fulvus,* "deep yellow," stock epithet of gold. Accordingly, he portrayed her as outstandingly beautiful and outstandingly greedy. Her lover associates the former trait with her name during the reconciliation of a quarrel: "Why, now my FULVIA lookes, like her bright name! / And is her selfe!" (II.348–49). He continues the association even while he complains: her beauty is kept "within locks, and barres, here,/ Like a fooles treasure." Fulvia accepts the equation and replies, "True, shee was a foole,/ When, first, shee shew'd it to a thiefe" (II.217–19). She thinks about and evaluates herself totally in terms of gold; she knows her face is her fortune, and her quarrel with her lover Curius is caused by his not giving sufficient money for value: his gifts have recently decreased; in enjoying her he is "a thiefe." She understands her worth and desires the outward sign of her inner predilections:

They shall all give, and pay well, that come here,
If they will have it: and that, jewells, pearle,
Plate, or round summes, to buy these. I'am not taken
With a cot-swan, or a high-mounting bull,
As foolish LEDA, and EUROPA were,
But the bright gold, with DANAE. (II.177–82)

12. Cf. Jonson's objection to Guillaume de Salluste Du Bartas, author of *La Sepmaine; ou, Creation du Monde* (1578), "that he thought not Bartas a Poet but a Verser, because he wrote not Fiction" *(CD,* 58–59).
13. Commentary on *C,* II, in HS, *10,* 132–33.

When she reveals Catiline's conspiracy to Cicero and urges Curius to second her, she tempts him with her favorite consideration: "Follow the fortune I ha' put you into:/ You may be something this way, and with safetie" (III.382–83).

Her lover's character is somewhat more complex. He is a weak man, committed in turn to various objects, insecure in each commitment. His dependence upon Fulvia appears at first to be solely physical, but the quarrel between them and his extreme joy in their reconciliation reveal an emotional dependence almost pathetic when one considers his lady's motivations. He is easily worked upon to be angry or sorrowful, as Fulvia well understands; and when she has revealed his political secrets to Cicero, Curius is quickly induced to repent. He becomes Cicero's spy, a part he performs better than desired, for he confirms an accusation of Caesar which Cicero does not follow up and which Caesar so resents that he requests assurance from Cicero that no reward will be paid Curius for his services. In view of his objective troubles with Fulvia, Cicero, and Caesar, increased by his troubled conscience and precarious emotional stability, it seems only natural that his name should be Curius, the care-full or troubled one.

If Curius is weighed down by the implications of his name, the ineffectual conspirator Lentulus is brought nearly to a halt by his. His name, diminutive of "slow, sluggish, immovable," proclaims to the world what everybody on both sides knows. His confederates nag him unceasingly: "You are too heavy, LENTULUS, and remisse" (III.224); "Why, LENTULUS, talke you so long? This time/ Had beene enough, t'have scatter'd all the starres" (IV.758–59). Catiline calls him "dull, stupide LENTULUS" (III.722); and when, just as expected, the conspiracy fails under his leadership, Caesar remarks resignedly, "I ever look'd for this of LENTULUS,/ When CATILINE was gone" (V.68–69), while Cicero observes, "I thought, when I had thrust out CATILINE,/ Neither the state, nor I, should need t'have fear'd/ LENTULUS sleepe here" (V.233–35). From the historian's point of view, Lentulus might have had a chance of success—but from that of the insightful poet, none whatever, as Jonson makes amply clear in his insistence upon "the sloth/ And sleepinesse of LENTULUS" (V.380–81).

Brisker and more successful in the concerns his name dictates is Lentulus' fellow conspirator Bestia, on whose behalf Catiline threatens one of his pageboys with a beating for being "somewhat modest" (I.505): "Arise, and shew/ But any least aversion i' your looke/ To him that bourds you next, and your throat opens" (I.510–12). One assumes that when Bestia bourds him again, he will find him more coming. Cautiously, Herford and Simpson remark that "the satyr nature of Bestia," not in Sallust (he "mentions the suspicion of such vice, but not at this point of the history"), "is apparently due to a misunderstanding of his name or a word-play upon it."[14]

To Jonson the construction of such correspondences was far more than word-play: it was part of the truthful framework into which his plays were built. Names do not so much expose the nature of the characters as show that exposure is inevitable. If a man of bestial desires is named Bestia, this "coincidence" goes to show that essentially no hypocrisy is possible. *"Man* is read in his face" *(D,* 522), and a name is a kind of verbal face. Indeed, the characters ·recognize the meaning of their own and one another's names. Cob in *Every Man in* speaks of himself as a herring, tracing his lineage back to a fish (I.4.1–32); Squire Tub requests as a masque *"A Tale of a Tub,* a storie of my selfe,/ You can expresse a Tub" (V.2.43–45); and Onion, hiding in a tree while Jaques exclaims upon his gold in the garden, "ô how sweet it smels," mutters to himself: "I mar'le he smels not *Onion,* being so neere it" *(CA,* IV.8.70–71).

These are trivial recognitions; one degree higher in importance are those which, like Curius' interpretation of Fulvia's name, enable characters to perceive when their fellows are or are not behaving according to their natural inclinations. But the most significant bring out the effect on the action of an unalterable cast of mind. Volpone repeatedly speaks of his dupes Voltore, Corbaccio, and Corvino in terms like "vulture . . . / Raven, and gor-crow, all my birds of prey" (I.2.88–89); and when he has had it given out that he is dead, Mosca accurately predicts that the first would-be heir to arrive will be "the vulture:/ He has the

14. Commentary on *C,* I.505–12, in HS, *10,* 130.

quickest sent" (V.2.108–09). Volpone's incomprehension of his role's limited potentialities is made plain as he interprets his name: "The *Foxe* fares ever best, when he is curst" (V.3.119). His interpretation contrasts with Mosca's, for the latter sees his patron on the path to destruction when "my FOXE/ Is out on his hole" and exposed to "the FOXE-trap" (V.5.6–7, 18).

In short, the names of the characters are no comparison, but a complete identification. Cob *is* a herring, Tub *is* a tub. The picture darkens when we realize that Voltore *is* a vulture, Volpone *is* a fox; they cannot escape the meanings of their names even if they try. Although in the earlier comedies Jonson handles this implication by never showing us such characters after they have reformed, as the years and plays pass and reformation becomes less frequent, he follows his system of naming nearer and nearer to its logical conclusion—a form of poetic predestination. In a play like *Volpone* or in a man like Lentulus this predestination results, if not in tragedy, at least in tragic rather than comicall satyre.

Predestination is a view ill at ease with the doctrine of man's recurring responsibility for evil, inherent in Jonson's concept of Nature as invariably good and truthful. One is bound to ask why man is to be brought to account for characteristics he can no more help than he can help his outer appearance—by which, apparently, he is also to be judged. There is a double answer.

In the first place, Jonson's names, although they do represent the entire potentiality of each of his characters, do not necessarily represent the entire potentiality of man. Jonson was undoubtedly well aware of the complexity of a "Paul" as opposed to a "Politique Would-be." Presumably the play's evil could have been averted by better moral choices on the part of the characters at some point prior to the beginning of the play, which would have prevented their ending up with such motivations in such an action. Their previous characters, which would have required different names, are of course irrelevant to a play concerned with what occurs when its personages have allowed themselves to become what the list of characters proclaims them to be.

From this point of view, the naming of *Volpone* is optimistic: the relegation of all malefactors to an animal level postulates a higher human plane which they fail to reach. The effect is similar to that of the names in Jonson's *Epigrams:* "On Court-Worme" (XV), "To Hornet" (LXXXVIII), "On Old Colt" (XXXIX), "To Sir Cod" (L). The subjects of these epigrams, taken together, make up a subhuman world like that of *Volpone.* That the vicious are not considered human implies a high standard of humanity, for only the man who gives himself over to his animal drives is inescapably doomed to evil and punishment. These are the men who direct toward base goals the "spirit, that may conforme them, actually,/ To *Gods* high figures, which they have in power." Such misapplication of divine gifts "Is sacrilege, of an unpardon'd greatnesse" *(CR,* V.4.645–46, 648). The high standard is upheld and represented by Celia and Bonario in *Volpone,* as it is in the *Epigrams* by such men as the Earl of Salisbury and the Earl of Suffolk; the former, like the latter, become not less but more than individuals, almost a copy of the divine pattern graciously granted to man.

> *Good men* are the Stars, the Planets of the Ages wherein they live, and illustrate the times. *God* did never let them be wanting to the world: As *Abel,* for an example, of Innocency; *Enoch* of Purity, *Noah* of Trust in Gods mercies, *Abraham* of Faith, and so of the rest.
>
> *(D,* 1100–04)

In *Volpone* the heavenly illumination does finally penetrate society and its judgment: man's animal elements are rejected, his spiritual worth reaffirmed.

The pessimistic side of this first answer is to be found in *The Alchemist.* Here, since good men are wanting to the world, the high standard cannot be applied. Nor is it implied, for the names of the charlatans and of the dupes are those of human qualities or human beings; one is even superhuman—the name of a false god, Mammon. These schemers are not vegetable like Onion and Juniper, not animal like Volpone and Mosca, not allegorical like Asotus and Anaides; they are human beings of a particular turn of mind. There is a difference also between them and a character like Meere-craft, personification of a vice ("*Wisedome* without *Honesty* is meere craft, and coosinage" [*D,* 89]). Subtle, Dapper, even Lovewit and Surly are not personifications but

persons described by the adjectives most suitable to their characters. So
Dol Common and Drugger are types of people, as a Sir Epicure is a type
of person.

This is equally true in *Epicoene,* but there the best men win, whereas
in *The Alchemist* there is only one better man, and he is worsted. To be
Morose is in any case more forgivable than to be Subtle: a man may be
subject to moroseness, but no man is subject to subtlety. The Alchemist's
name and those of his associates emphasize the greater burden of personal responsibility in this play, a burden no one wants to assume. In
their names lies the explanation of their incapacity as human beings.

Even Surly is not made of the true metal: surliness is not enough
with which to approach the truth; one needs Clemency, Manliness, a
Critical sense of life.[15] In Surly, Truewit's case is reversed, for while
Surly's actions are effective enough, his motivation is at fault, ruining his
chances for lasting success before he starts. He is a kind of faintly
drawn Macilente, devoted to honesty for the wrong reasons: Surly is
not envious, but he is intolerant and bad-tempered. In fact, to be Surly
is not so far from being Morose; both need the saving grace of good
spirit. Lovewit, who has good spirit, has not Surly's devotion to honesty;
qualities are divided among the characters of this play, which, unlike any
other, even at the end contains nothing approaching a complete man.

The rogues and fools of this world are not punished because there is
no one to punish them. Lovewit, upon whose shoulders the responsibility
would seem squarely to fall, shrugs it off by applying aesthetic, intellectual, and sensual, rather than moral, criteria. He is a Falsewit rather
than a Truewit, bearing a certain resemblance to the witty but immoral
Ovid, who could also overlook much for a well-turned woman or jest.
But there is no Augustus or Virgil to put Lovewit in his place. That
inferior position has become in *The Alchemist* the top of the hierarchy.

The hierarchy, in its broadest sense, is a key concept in Jonson's
work; herein lies the second answer to the debate between predestination
and personal responsibility. The proper arrangement of society is a
reflection of that eternal Proper Arrangement brought about by divine

15. Possessed by Justice Clement *(EI),* Manly *(DA),* and Crites *(CR).*

forces; it supersedes, therefore, any concern of or for the individual. An individual whose character causes him to disrupt the ethical order of society or to aid in the establishment of an ethically unacceptable order is to be condemned. This is a view leaning rather backward than forward: it looks toward the Middle Ages more steadily than toward the twentieth century. One can find an outstanding example of it in Chaucer's Pardoner, whose offenses against man and God are not excused by being—as they are more than implied to be—the result of the physical impotence which has produced complex twistings in his character. Their source does not alter the fact that the twistings are evil and the Pardoner a vicious man: moral limitation is culpable however it comes about. The view, though perhaps somewhat distasteful to a psychology-minded generation, has a certain logical justification, particularly for a playwright: If one subtracts the character for which a man is not responsible, what remains to which to assign or refuse responsibility?

Most of Jonson's plays end with an arrangement of society in which the best person is most highly valued—a copy of that divine evaluation in which God, the unalloyed Good, stands at the head of an order that descends through men (with great potential for good) to beasts and plants. But in *The Alchemist* the scapegraces and outlaws are integrated into a hierarchy of amused hypocrisy, for man is no longer capable of making any pattern other than a false one. The inability to establish a valid final pattern is the most telling judgment this society makes on itself. What Nature does, man undoes: she reveals the truth, and he covers it up again.

The Truth of Circumstance

Just as man in action works with Nature to establish a pattern of greater overall importance than any man within it, so the artist works with Nature to establish his imitation of her pattern. Inevitably, the total framework of Jonson's plays—that is, those elements on which the action is built: the characters' names, the settings, the principles of plot construction—is more significant in terms of metaphysical truth than any individual character or action. Not that the distinction is entirely logical, for an order must consist of things ordered; but for purposes of analysis, it is possible to separate these from the principles of ordering. Jonson's view of the artist's duty was strict: "Wee must not goe about like men anguish'd, and perplex'd, for vitious affectation of praise: but . . . seeke the consonancy, and concatenation of Truth" (D, 2106–15). The concatenation of Truth is the eternal framework within which specific events take place; it is of more lasting significance than any set of occurrences. That is why Jonson's plays, although varying in plot, vary scarcely at all in plot structure. He was not content with exhorting men to reform, even by the indirect means of didactic drama. Rather, he wished to show them why they ought to reform, by demonstrating the forces toward Truth operating in the universe itself, with which men cannot hope to be in harmony unless their own drives are similar: "For without truth all the Actions of mankind, are craft, malice, or what you will" (D, 534–35). In order to fulfill the poet's responsibility toward his fellowman, Jonson set the practical truth of believable action against the metaphysical truth of natural law. Since his characters, who do not perceive the latter, act upon craft, malice, or what you will, the play as a whole provides a clear view of what the world has become, juxtaposed against the framework which shows what it essentially is.

The most important implications of Jonson's names—that Nature works to align appearance with reality, that man's responsibility is to do likewise for the good of society, and that failure to do so is entirely the fault of man—are all supported by the structure of Jonson's plots—specifically, by the singular dearth of coincidence and by its function when it occurs. Coincidence is Nature moving without the aid of man; and there is not a single instance in Jonson of coincidence playing into the hands of villainy or folly.

On the contrary, in Jonson's work coincidence operates invariably to the disadvantage of the schemers and to the advantage, whether there are schemers or not, of the truth. When a group of related but disguised people assembles by chance under the same roof, the result is mutual recognition of family ties (NI, CA); when a lover returns home along the same road by which his lady is being abducted, the result is her rescue and a false friend's discovery and reform *(CA);* when a man arrives at his own or another's house sooner than expected, he brings about the confutation of hitherto successful villainy.[16] The closest approach to an occurrence outside the control of the protagonists which furthers the cause of evil is the collapse of a portion of the cave in which Tiberius is eating, an accident which enables Sejanus to save the Emperor by propping up "the remayning ruines" with his own body (IV.47–60). This action restores Sejanus very briefly to favor, but the interlude is so short that one feels the incident to be rather a foreshadowing of Sejanus' destruction, when he will not be able to stave off the fatal collapse of his shelter, than the source of any real gain for his plots. His brief period of renewed favor seems to sap his strength rather than increase it. We feel that "that which hapned . . . with great gratulation, and applause, how it hath lifted him, but a step higher to his ruine! As if hee stood before, where hee might fall safely" *(D,* 963–66).

But altogether the most remarkable feature of coincidence in Ben Jonson's plays is its rarity. It is astonishing to see again and again how minute a part is played by any factor not derived from the original situation by logical development. As Swinburne observes, "There is nothing accidental in the work of Ben Jonson."[17] There may be tiresome scenes, there may be superfluous scenes, but there are no illogical scenes. Such extreme regularity of structure is the more surprising when one considers the surface confusion of his plots, most of which are impossible to remember in any detail. It is a real feat to explain how the various characters in *Bartholomew Fair* happen to arrive at the Fair simultaneously or indeed what they have to do there in the first place, or what inspires the reversals and rereversals in the final courtroom scenes of Volpone, or why exactly the unfortunate Dapper spends an act and three scenes in the Alchemist's privy.

16. Corvino and Celia arrive too soon at Volpone's house, permitting the concealed Bonario to overhear Volpone's attempt to seduce Celia; Lovewit returns to London before the alchemical trio in his house expects him, causing the flight of Dol and Subtle and the confession of Face.

17. Algernon Charles Swinburne, *A Study of Ben Jonson* (New York, 1889), p. 9.

Within this apparent chaos the strictest order reigns. There is always
a reason. Dapper's sojourn in "*Fortunes* privy lodgings" (*A,* III.5.79) is
necessary to Subtle, Dol, and Face, because Sir Epicure Mammon has
arrived for a previously promised conference with Dol, to whom Dapper
is about to convey devotional offerings (he thinks she is the Queen of
the Fairies and will make his fortune). In order to lose neither Dapper's
minor nor Sir Epicure's major contribution to their loot, the three rogues
must stow Dapper temporarily in the privy, where he stays quietly
forgotten (gagged with gingerbread which he does not eat because he
has been told he must approach the Queen fasting) until, having at last
consumed his gag "to stay my stomach," he calls out with anguished
perseverance: "For gods sake, when wil her *Grace* be at leisure?"
(V.4.5–6, V.3.65). In this apparent confusion, organized with smooth
efficiency, Sir Epicure's lechery, previously worked upon by Face, ensures his all-too-punctual arrival; the attempt of the rogues to carry out
all their plans consistently, ensured by their greed and love of intrigue,
necessarily requires the temporary elimination of Dapper; and Dapper's
anxiety for the favor of the Queen ensures his silence.

The trial scenes in *Volpone* are rooted with equal strength in the
soil of foregoing events; their profusion of accusation and counter-
accusation, reformation and counterreformation, is merely the branching
of one well-watered tree. Voltore's eagerness to support Volpone's deception, being based on greed for Volpone's favor and inheritance, naturally
vanishes when the latter is believed dead, with Mosca his heir, and returns when belief in the status quo is revived. Volpone's fortunate
presence depends upon his previous assumption of a disguise, and his
expectation that Mosca will support him, upon his previous assumptions concerning Mosca. But Mosca, in possession of Volpone's fortune,
has become self-supporting. The entire courtroom situation, and thus
the entire denouement, stems from Volpone's attempt on Celia and his
subsequent trick on the gulls—that is, from his character as voluptuary
and trickster and from the greed of his gulls—that is, from the central
concerns of the plot.

Even in that most complex of Jonson's plays, *Bartholomew Fair,* the
pattern proves the same as ever. From the four corners of London's

earth the protagonists have come to the Fair to be undeceived and joined into a wiser society. The Littlewit contingent is linked (by the marriage of Littlewit's mother-in-law, Dame Purecraft, and Quarlous) to the two young gallants Quarlous and Winwife, who are joined (by Winwife's engagement to Grace) to the faction of her erstwhile fiancé Cokes and to her guardian Justice Overdo. The result is the hand-linked chain of the dance of life, in which Justice Overdo leads the procession winding in and out under the arches made by the arms of its own members: the mismatched Mistress Grace is suitably joined to Winwife, who had been unsuitably courting Dame Purecraft, who has married— because wedded bliss with a madman has been foretold her—Quarlous, who has disguised himself as a madman[18] who had once been injured by Justice Overdo, who has in pity given the supposed madman what he desires: a signed blank warrant, which has been used by Quarlous to free Grace, whose license to marry Cokes has been stolen for Quarlous by a young pickpocket, who has been mistaken for an honest man worthy of protection by Overdo, who is interested in exposing the moral debilitation of Mrs. Littlewit to her husband at the puppet show, which all the protagonists attend and which is the reason that has brought half of them to the Fair. The chain is unbreakable; nothing occurs which would not logically occur, given the characters whom proximity forces to interact. Even the turmoil of Bartholomew Fair can be reduced to a natural development of events resulting in revelation of the truth.

So minimal is the role of chance in Jonson's plays that more often than not an occurrence apparently coincidental proves to depend upon unavoidable motivation. Even, for example, the appearance at the New Inn of the Host's daughter (unaware of the relationship, of course) with her company of merrymakers is based on her heredity: she is specifically said to have inherited her father's madcap temperament (I.5.65–66), which would as naturally lead her to choose as site for her revels an inn called The Light Heart as it would lead her father to give

18. In order to get a sight of the name marked out for Grace on a paper by the real madman, whose arbitrary decision is to settle her preferences on Quarlous or Winwife.

his inn that name. It is just because they are father and daughter that the inn reunites them. To take a yet stronger case, the temperament of Corvino and the previous suggestions of Mosca, rather than mere coincidence, lead the eager husband to arrive early for the sacrifice of his wife upon the double altar of his covetousness and Volpone's bed.

In fact, within the entire Jonson canon of seventeen highly complicated plays, there are no more than three or four unmotivated occurrences or coincidences. Once the situation and characters are accepted as given, the development is that of a geometric system from its axioms. Although we may occasionally wish that the instructor had refrained from adding this or that theorem, he never adds a theorem that cannot be derived from the postulates.

This amazing tightness of construction prompted Dryden to name Jonson originator and teacher, in the English drama, of "the copiousness and well-knitting of the intrigues," his criteria for which are eminently applicable to Jonson:[19]

> If then the parts are managed so regularly, that the beauty of the whole be kept entire, and that the variety become not a perplexed and confused mass of accidents, you will find it infinitely pleasing to be led in a labyrinth of design, where you see some of your way before you, yet discern not the end till you arrive at it.

Two of his three examples of this kind of construction are taken from Jonson, and the discussion is followed by an examen of "the pattern of a perfect play": Jonson's *Epicoene*. Coleridge, on the other hand, prefers *The Alchemist* as his example of one of the "most perfect plots ever planned," while Swinburne, admiring the same techniques that called forth Dryden's praise, chooses *Every Man in* as the acme of their success: it is "so blameless and flawless a piece of work; so free from anything that might as well or better be dispensed with, so simply and thoroughly compact in workmanship and in result."[20] To Dryden's and Coleridge's

19. John Dryden, "An Essay of Dramatic Poesy," in Ker, *Essays*, p. 78, lines 9–11; p. 73, lines 12–18; p. 79, line 12.
20. Samuel Taylor Coleridge, "Table Talk," July 5, 1834, in *Coleridge's Literary Criticism*, ed. J. W. Mackail (London, 1908), p. 153; Swinburne, *Ben Jonson*, p. 14.

instances of plays exemplary in design, he justly adds *The Staple of News,* too often considered one of the "dotages." Jonson was a poet's poet; those who understood and sympathized with his purpose also understood and sympathized with his achievement.

For Jonson the creation of "perfect plots" unfolding according to the laws of necessity was aesthetically desirable because morally true: the universe is so constructed that, moved by inherent promptings, "Mischiefes feed/ Like beasts, till they be fat, and then they bleed" *(V, V.12.150–51).* But there is a point beyond which such unaided development cannot go. Once Jonson's premises have been fully worked out, it remains for the observers to decide what to do about the system revealed. Whether the bleeding beast is to be allowed to bleed to death or is rather to be recovered depends upon its keeper. Man must complete what Nature begins, for society, though the natural conclusion of revelations about man's relation to other men, is made by man and not by Nature. The personal responsibility of man for his position on the side of good or evil is clear in every one of Jonson's plays, from the earliest to the last.

So in *The Case Is Altered* the course of Nature decrees that Count Ferneze's friend should take Ferneze's long-lost son Camillo prisoner along with the only man who can prove Camillo's identity; the course of Nature guarantees that Paulo will encounter his beloved at the very spot and moment of her attack by his false friend; but judgment—and forgiveness—of the friend's offenses rests with Paulo, as recognition of his own overausterity toward his unknown son rests with the Count. The course of Nature ensures that Onion and Juniper will reveal themselves as the thieves of Jaques' money, while Jaques reveals his own identity and misdeeds; for Onion and Juniper, being what they are, are bound to turn their affectations and aspirations into an attempt to pass for men of fashion once they acquire money, just as Jaques is bound to make frenziedly heedless attempts to recover his money once he has lost it. But the punishment of Onion and Juniper and the pardon of Jaques are reserved to the offended parties.[21] Similarly, Nature, albeit moving at a

21. The party considered as offended by Onion and Juniper is their master the Count rather than Jaques, since the latter has been discredited not only as worthy judge but even as legitimate possessor of the money.

jerky pace, makes certain that Awdrey *(TT)*, courted by four men with any one of whom she would be equally mismatched, is accidentally married at last to a far more suitable fifth; but it remains for Squire Tub to set the example of forgiveness toward this secret marriage which has dashed his own hopes, an example adopted by all the others concerned; and it is Squire Tub, in this respect like Justice Clement, who makes his pronouncements palatable to his neighbors with a banquet.

This general rule of play structure and working ethics holds true throughout Jonson's work, assuming greater importance in the Comicall Satyres, in which the power of final judgment is given to characters of genuine significance, and in the mature and later plays, in which use of this power judges the judge. Never in Jonson does Nature herself step in and conclude the problem. No lover accidentally kills a beloved, no devil arrives to claim the hero's soul, no witches' prophecy proves true. The only devil to appear in Jonson is quite unable either to influence or to judge human actions *(DA);* in fact, the behavior of men has more effect on the fate of this supernatural being (Pug is entirely discredited with his superiors) than any supernatural force on the actions of men. The final works conform to the same design: in *The Staple of News* the judge is old Peniboy; in *The New Inn* the judge is the Host, assisted by some of his guests. The revelatory denouement of *The Magnetic Lady* turns upon the eminently natural occurrence of the birth of a natural child to the well-named Placentia, an event blessed only in that it leads to the discovery that Placentia, although magnetic in her own way, is not the niece of Lady Loadstone and has therefore by her behavior forfeited no inheritance for herself or anybody else; but the situation is resolved by the decisions of Lady Loadstone and her two aides, Captain Ironside and Mr. Compass. Even Jonson's last play, of which we have only the groundwork, shows the same blueprint: the disguises of the witch and her kidnapping of the sad shepherd's sweetheart are clearly to be exposed in part through the natural intelligence and loving confidence of Robin Hood and Marian, while the presence in the cast of *"The Reconciler. Reuben,* A devout Hermit," suggests a projected ending of the Justice Clement type.

The Truthful Setting

Against this metaphysical theme of inevitable revelation which invariably precedes the coda of judgment, Jonson has placed the counterpoint of naturalistic action—those speeches and events which have earned him the dubious honor of the title "realist." Here he mirrors the society around him, placing beside the unchanging divine form the decaying human content. The glass is turned toward Nature in the framework of his plays and toward life in their action, bringing both into focus in a likeness of Truth.[22]

Nowhere is the relation and contrast clearer than in his treatment of settings. There are two sorts of settings in Jonson: the "natural" and the man-made. The first is the product of the poet's mind, operating on his material as Nature does on hers; the second, the product of the mind of one or more of the characters, operating like the imagination of a false poet against the order around him, inspired by an arrogant confidence in his own powers to challenge Nature's great work with his little countermechanism.

Jonson's representation of natural settings is, like his representation of names, a symbolic rather than a literal rendition of practical truth. In ironic real life, jealous of any visible correspondence between its inner and outer composition, corruption is more likely to inhabit the corner of Church and Chapel Streets than to confine itself to an intersection named, say, Hellfire Crossroads. To the wide-eyed Sunday sightseer, Sodom Lane reveals itself as a quiet Connecticut residential area,[23] teeming not with perverted sensuality but with children and bicycles. This sort of inconsistency Jonson's world does not permit: the Sodom Lane of any play of his, whether it be called Venice or Bartholomew Fair, contains all the vice and folly its name implies. The audience knows, even before the characters have decided, what form the action will take. There is no

22. For the distinction between "Nature" and "naturalistic," see above, pp. 9 and 55 (Nature) and the discussion of "practical truth," above, p. 54.
23. Just outside Derby.

realistic nonsense about it: Augustan Rome is just, Gargaphie will tolerate only heavenly perfection, Venice is corrupt. As in the case of Jonson's names, we are dealing with a clarification rather than a distortion of practical truth. There is no reason why action should not correspond to setting; Jonson removes the misleading cases in which it does not, and leaves the essential cases in which it does, to show from one more vantage point that appearance and reality are in the end the same. Such trimming of excess material is the artist's privilege, even his task. Jonson, having the advantage of a place to stand, moves the world to a site appropriate to its action.

Mention has already been made of the significance of *Poetaster's* setting, which, by invoking the authority of Augustus and his poet-counselors, invokes the authority of discovered and established poetic— that is, metaphysical—truth, along with the practical truth of history. We can be certain before the Emperor speaks a word that neither impure nor untalented poetry, nor blasphemy nor slander will be tolerated in this golden era of poetic knowledge. Equal certainty, though of quite the opposite sort, is provided by the setting of *Volpone*. The Elizabethan audience had only to be told that it was to behold Venice, that floating Bower of Bliss, in order to anticipate the character of the citizenry. To the Elizabethans the courtesan of the Adriatic was the emblem of *cupiditas* in all its forms, the very incarnation of the city of Juvenal's sixth satire, in which one craving becomes representative of all; in Juvenal the original *cupiditas* is sexual, in *Volpone* monetary, but in both the combination of physical and fiscal makes a striking case for human judgment. The scene of *Volpone's* action lends credence to the events that unfold; but more important, events and setting corroborate one another to indicate that inner vice gives itself away by outer manifestations. If the characters really hoped to dupe the spectators into believing their deceptions, they should never have made the mistake of living in Venice. They ought to have emigrated to Gargaphie or taken up temporary residence at The Light Heart, in either of which places action must evidently be directed toward goodness and truth. But Jonson would never have let them in. His object was precisely not to dupe the spectators but to reveal the truth to them—not the truth about the characters, which in all but one of the major plays is known from the beginning, but the truth about Nature and her workings. If he showed them a court headed by Cynthia, goddess of purity and truth, it was in order to present the vision of a society available to man in which the guiding principles are purity and truth, in which reformation of miscreants becomes philosophically necessary because such an ideal "exerts a supernatural force," and "in Cynthia's presence each fool . . . adapts himself to the divine order which the goddess automatically imposes."[24]

The application of this vision is necessarily left to the spectators, just as the application of the knowledge gained within the play is necessarily left to its characters. The position of the audience at the end of the play is analogous to that of the characters when the truth has been revealed. But just as there were those in the audience who preferred deception to understanding and criticized the structure of Jonson's plays (for it was as such a preference that Jonson, convinced of the aim of his art, saw their criticism), there are those characters in Jonson who actively pit themselves against the truthful microcosm within which they act, by constructing a shelter against beneficent Nature from within which they assail her, rather than she them, with storms. The outstanding characteristics of this microcosm within a microcosm are always that it is artificial and man-made, that it is the creation of deceit or wrongheadedness, and that it is bound to be destroyed by its own violence. The deception or wrongheaded whim for which it is a means and a protection fails as soon as the attempt is made to attack the real world by carrying the fraud or idiosyncrasy beyond its artificial confines—and the attempt is inevitably made. Such man-made microcosms are the settings-within-settings of Jaques' house and grounds in *The Case Is Altered,* Fitz-Dottrell's estate in *The Devil Is an Ass,* Peniboy Senior's home in *The Staple of News,* to some extent Ursula's tent in *Bartholomew Fair* and Placentia's sickroom in *The Magnetic Lady,* and, of much greater importance, Volpone's bedroom, Morose's soundproof house, and the alchemical workshop of Lovewit's mansion.

These are the burrows within whose sheltering warmth falsehood and

24. Campbell, *Comicall Satyre,* p. 105.

obsession breed. As long as Jaques can cache his stolen gold in his own garden and his stolen daughter in his own house, both his deceit and his obsession are safe. Rachel and the money are not only the spoils of his betrayal of Lord Chamount, they are the lasting symbols of it. As spoils they serve little purpose; as symbols, a great deal. Jaques makes no use of his money or of his supposed daughter: he spends none of the gold, nor does he attempt to increase his store or Rachel's position by, for example, marrying the girl well—though nothing would have been easier, to judge by the eagerness with which at least four men apparently above her in rank besiege father and daughter for her hand. He does not enjoy the presence of his gold, since he is in constant fear of its being stolen; he does not enjoy the presence of his supposed daughter, whom he wishes out of the way "That I might live alone once with my gold" (II.1.25), and whom he stole from her family not out of affection but out of pity for the child, "Because it lov'd me so, that it would leave/ The nurse her selfe, to come into mine armes,/ And had I left it, it would sure have dyed" (II.1.38–40). He sees the two as objects linked together by their association with the most important and most shattering event in his life. His only impulse is to hug them both to him; his only fear, that they may be stolen—a psychologically valid disguise for his guilt and apprehension of being found out. Interestingly but not surprisingly, the only portion of the ill-gotten money he uses is spent on Rachel. This connection, accurate in psychological terms, becomes accurate in practical terms also when the double theft of Rachel and the gold precipitates discovery of his deception. The notable point in this discovery is that Jaques himself brings it about: it is he who objectifies his psychological quirk when his need to recover the symbols of his guilty secret leads him to betray the connection to other men. Everything happens as he has dimly felt it will, because his dim feelings cause it to do so. He, who has previously spoken to his gold in the privacy of his garden as "my deere child" (III.5.16), now shouts to the world the identification he cannot help making: "thou hast made away my child, thou hast my gold:/ . . ./ The thiefe is gone: my gold's gone, *Rachel's* gone" (V.5.18–20). The destruction of his cozy, safe, symbolic world brings with it the destruction of his fear, destroyed as soon as it is realized. When Jaques understands the force of his new position, he accepts the fact that "the case is altered" and proceeds to make a full confession of his own accord, setting himself free from his obsession and justifying Chamount's forgiveness and gift of the recovered money. The other deceptions which have flourished on his grounds similarly wither when they are transplanted into harsher air. Juniper and Onion are successful in making off with the buried money, but the moment they attempt to put it to use, they are discovered and punished. Angelo is able to deceive Rachel into thinking him a faithful friend to her lover as long as they converse only at her home; the moment he attempts to put his infatuation for her into action by abducting her, he exposes his plot to failure and his character to the eyes of his friend. Honest error may hold sway for a while in the world at large: Ferneze may fail to recognize his son; but deceit is safe only on Jaques' property. His house and grounds become symbolic of the limited, man-made scope accorded to falsehood.

Fitz-Dottrell in his preoccupation with his wife and his fortune would run Jaques a close second in obsession, except that his motivation is nothing more forceful than native idiocy. He consequently yields second place to Peniboy Senior, whose attachment to the Lady Pecunia, so great that he has kept her "close prisoner, under twenty bolts—/ And forty padlocks—" (*SN*, IV.3.33–34), turns to madness when she leaves him and he ventures out to seek her. Her very departure is, paradoxically, the result of his possessiveness: he allows her to leave with his supposedly rich nephew in the hope of converting the latter's interest in Pecunia to pecuniary interest. The possessiveness of both old Peniboy and Fitz-Dottrell is successful as long as they can keep its objects strictly within their control, which means within their homes. While Fitz-Dottrell's wife can be spied upon by the servants or her husband, even her balcony scene with Wittipol, in which *"He growes more familiar in his Courtship, playes with her paps, kisseth her hands, &c."* (*DA*, II.6, s.d. to 71–78), makes Fitz-Dottrell feel only that "I ha' beene vex'd a little, with a toy" (II.8.2). Out-and-out cuckoldry is all he fears, and this he can prevent as long as he does not permit his wife to leave the house. Nor are his webs of social and financial ambition, which he spins with the cheater Meere-craft's projects as stimulus, in danger of being swept away so long as he decorates only the corners of his own rooms with them; but, as in *The Case Is Altered,* the threads of obsession and deception break when stretched over a larger space. Fitz-Dottrell puts his wife and money in Wittipol's hands when his desire to prepare her for social advancement leads him to send her, bearing valuable gifts, to take deportment lessons from a "Spanish lady"—who is Wittipol in disguise. Like Jaques and old Peniboy, Fitz-Dottrell sets up the conditions for the situation he most fears, through the very motives which cause him to fear it: covetous ambition and covetous uxoriousness. At the same time, Meere-craft's attempts to cozen him collapse because of Wittipol's devious counteractivity, while Wittipol's own hopes are dashed by Mrs. Fitz-Dottrell's reticence. Neither Wittipol nor Meere-craft can extend into the outside world the success he has had in Fitz-Dottrell's house.

In each of these situations it is the very obsession of the ruler of that artificial world, the household, which brings on his disaster; it is the persistence of his visitors in the deceptions that succeed within his house that ensures their ruin. All the participants overreach themselves, and their overreaching is psychologically inevitable. The small scope of effectiveness Jonson grants to vice is intimately connected with the brief duration he allows it, his belief that "No lye ever growes old," that when mischiefs have fed themselves fat they will bleed, since they are by nature insatiable. This is equally true for the mischief of obsession and the mischief of deception. Placentia's sickroom and Ursula's tent differ from the artificial microcosms already discussed in being rest homes for temporarily inactive vices rather than shelters for obsession, but the end result for their inhabitants is the same. When Placentia emerges from her confinement to pretend that it has not taken place, her social rank—and influence —soon prove as insubstantial as her maidenhood, for she is discovered to be the waiting-woman's daughter, exchanged in the cradle with her young mistress. Her true character, safe in the bedroom, cannot endure the stress of parlor life. Like the sharpers in the Fair, she is seen for what she is when she ventures beyond her natural habitat; although the sharpers have no punishment meted out to them, they too are unmasked when they go into action outside Ursula's tent.

Vice, according to Jonson, is a sensitive hothouse plant: it cannot bear the wind of open fields. Such a view places on men the obligation not to live in glass houses which protect poisonous blooms; those who do must beware of the splintering walls. Jaques, Fitz-Dottrell, Peniboy, Placentia —even the Fair's cheaters—escape serious injury. They have done no great harm, and they incur none. In those great plays, however, in which the artificial microcosm assumes its full symbolic value—*Epicoene, Volpone, The Alchemist*—destruction of a man-made nature by the real Nature means the end of a carefully constructed personal identity. In these plays maintenance of identity clearly depends upon opposition to the order of Nature, and the artificial microcosm is not merely a location but a specific expression of its maker, revealing in its physical details his psychological characteristics and his anti-natural aspirations.

The little world of Morose, for example, is determined by his desire for silence. His monomania "has made him devise a roome, with double walls, and treble seelings; the windores close shut, and calk'd: and there he lives by candle-light" *(SW*, I.1.184–86). Everything about Morose is as artificial as his light; his house, his way of life, his conversation, all must conform to his private design or they will not serve. His servant "waits on him . . . in tennis-court socks, or slippers sol'd with wooll" (I.1.188–89), and answers his master by signs only (II.1.5–7), for all conversation afflicts Morose—except his own, which issues in speeches often lasting some page and a half in print. His need for silence and his need for speech unite to form a need for unnatural treatment of language, which to Jonson is indicative of a need for the unnatural in all things, since *"Language* most shewes a man: . . . It springs out of the most retired, and inmost parts of us, and is the Image of the Parent of it, the mind" *(D,* 2031–33). Morose's habits of speech have shut him into an intellectual and spiritual microcosm which his surroundings precisely mirror. The better to shut out external Nature, his house has "a thicke quilt, or flock-bed, on the outside of the dore" (I.1.188). When someone does venture in, even if he comes with Morose's permission, he is ejected in the shortest possible order. In just the same way, Morose is intent upon ejecting from his concern whoever has a natural claim upon him, in order to preserve his spiritual silence and his moral monologue. Specifically, he is bent upon withholding from his natural kin, Sir Dauphine Eugenie, his rightful inheritance, and to encompass this end he attempts to turn an even closer natural relationship into an anti-natural paradox: he arranges a marriage which by its very terms will constitute a rejection. His wife is to be as un-natural as the rest of his life: she must be a self-contradiction, a silent woman. Morose robs even the most intimate bond between human beings of its possibilities for communication, deliberately cutting himself off from all human contact with a gesture more striking than, but no different in kind from, his previous regulation of his environment. *"Convivae nec muti, nec loquaces sunto" (LC,* 13) was Jonson's dictum. Morose, mutus et loquax, scorns the very concept of companionship. He rejects, he can-not abide, the fellowship of man—no, nor woman neither.

Here his obsession, according to the familiar design, overreaches itself and brings about his downfall—with the variation that he draws into his artificial world someone who does not belong there, instead of going out into the natural world where he does not belong. In requiring a natural human being to live in his artificial habitat, Morose imports a beneficial snake into his papier-mâché paradise and opens the portals to his unde-sired salvation. Since he is willing to assume the greatest possible unnatu-ralness in order to preserve his solitude, when he discovers that his wife is talkative he attempts to dissolve his marriage by pleading impotence. That this implies the ultimate degree of severance from his fellow human beings is made clear by the form of his statement: "I am no man" (V.4.44). His fortunate fall is precipitated by the revelation that in fact his wife is no woman but a boy in disguise. Morose is hereupon forced to endure not only the company of the merrymakers who have invaded his house but the bestowal of part of his money on the rightful heir and—most unac-customed of all—the emotion of gratitude toward his nephew, to whom he declares: "Thou art my restorer. Here, I deliver . . . my deed. If there bee a word in it lacking, or writ with false orthographie, I protest before —I will not take the advantage" (V.4.200–03). Some men are born to communicate, some achieve communication, some have communication thrust upon them. Morose, as one of the latter, must finally admit the power of that which is natural, including man's imagination when aligned with Nature rather than against her, to overcome that which is unnatural: silence, self-preoccupied speech, denial of ties with other human beings.

He is, after all, a man, and he is not impotent; like every other man, he possesses the power to uphold or to contravene the order of Nature—the power of good and evil.

Volpone uses this power to more pernicious ends than Morose. He not only wishes to cut himself off from other human beings, he wishes to cut other human beings off from one another—husband from wife, father from son. Like a spider in the center of his web of intrigue, he sits waiting to destroy; but the moment he ventures out, he too is doomed. His appearance as mountebank in a public square has the immediate effect of fetching him a sound drubbing, along with the more far-reaching effect of causing him to covet Celia, his attempt on whom eventually brings down that sounder legal drubbing which ends the play.

Volpone's imitation of Scoto of Mantua, a man with a supposedly health-giving essence to bestow upon the perspicacious buyer, is an exact parallel to his imitation of a man about to bequeath the blessing of wealth to the highest bidder. His performance as health-giver is an extension of his already virtuoso performance as wealth-giver. The essence he promises, whether embodied in Scoto's medicine or his own money, is equivalent to the oil of which Mosca speaks in Act I:

> MOS. Alas, sir, I but doe, as I am taught;
> Follow your grave instructions; give 'hem wordes;
> Powre oyle into their eares: and send them hence.
>
> VOLP. 'Tis true, 'tis true. What a rare punishment
> Is avarice, to it self? MOS. I, with our help, sir. (I.4.139–43)

It is a rare punishment because it results in the specific sort of self-deception which Volpone's "oyle" nourishes:

> So many cares, so many maladies,
> So many feares attending on old age,
> . . .
> . . . their limbs faint,
> Their senses dull, their seeing, hearing, going,
> All dead before them; yea, their very teeth,

Their instruments of eating, fayling them:
Yet this is reckon'd life! Nay, here was one,
Is now gone home, that wishes to live longer!
Feels not his gout, nor palsie, faines himselfe
Yonger, by scores of yeeres, flatters his age,
With confident belying it, hopes he may
With charmes, like Æson, have his youth restor'd:
And with these thoughts so battens, as if fate
Would be as easily cheated on, as he. (I.4.144–58)

The song by which Volpone as mountebank attempts to sell his medicine leaves no doubt that the nostrum is the same oil Volpone peddles at home:

You that would last long, list to my song,
Make no more coyle, but buy of this oyle.
Would you be ever faire? and yong?
Stout of teeth? and strong of tongue?
Tart of palat? quick of eare?
Sharpe of sight? of nostrill cleare?
Moist of hand? and light of foot?
(Or I will come neerer to 't)
Would you live free from all diseases?
Doe the act, your mistris pleases;
Yet fright all aches from your bones?
Here's a med'cine, for the nones. (II.2.192–203)

These are, as the striking parallels with Volpone's earlier speech confirm, the impossible and immoral goals of self-deluding men,[25] seeking not the source of natural health but the fountain of youth. Volpone's attempt to extend his "help" to his entire society causes in the long run the failure of all his schemes and the destruction of his manner of life. The public will not, in the end, buy his oil; instead, they will beat and expel him. The

25. Aptly enough, Volpone himself is said to have been "recovered" by Scoto's oil when it was poured into his ears (II.6.22–23). Of course this is a lie (by Mosca to Corvino), but like most of the other lies about Volpone's health, it is also a symbolic truth.

mountebank scene is a complete miniature statement of the play's major theme.

Volpone's second venture into the outside world leads directly to the denouement. Like Morose and the others, he overreaches himself. Not content with feeding the hopes of his dupes and taking their money, he wishes also to enjoy their disappointment. He is himself too greedy. Once having abandoned, because of his main vice, the burrow that shelters it, Volpone the Magnifico becomes but one more example of the extreme limitation of a vicious character's range of action, which expresses both the extreme limitation of his range of values and the optimistically small area of effectiveness Jonson grants them. The morally sick man is automatically in quarantine: he cannot infect the whole town.

In *The Alchemist,* however, moral disease is endemic rather than epidemic. "The absolutely unqualified and unrelieved rascality of every agent . . .—unless an exception should be made in favour of the unfortunate though enterprising Surly—is . . . a mark of comparative baseness in the dramatic metal,"[26] Swinburne opined. It is indeed a mark of baseness in the metal of the characters, which no amount of alchemical effort could possibly turn into gold, but it is far from being a "note of inferiority" in the play—only in the world the play represents. Swinburne seems to sense what the characters' names suggest, in spite of the play's lightness of touch: *The Alchemist* is a cynical play, far less optimistic than *Volpone,* which has often been said to border on tragedy. But tragedy is not necessarily pessimistic; and it is the hilarious *Alchemist* whose laughter takes for granted the decadent state of man. The dupes of Subtle, Face, and Dol are "Puritan and shopkeeping scoundrels," clearly "viler if less villainous figures than the rapacious victims of Volpone." No one reforms or exiles them at the end, as we have come to expect in Jonson's dramas; they do not seem to be worth the saving. Most important of all, the villains themselves get off scot free except for the loss of their loot.

Yet their villainy is metaphysically worse than any we have seen so far. While Morose denies Nature and imposes upon her his own artifices,

26. Quotations in this paragraph are from Swinburne, *Ben Jonson,* pp. 35–36.

and Volpone recognizes Nature but opposes her through the greed in himself and others, Subtle, in a criminally misdirected Herculean gesture, attempts to turn the course of Nature so that it will wind in his direction. The basic belief of alchemy is that Nature works toward perfection, of which gold is the material symbol, being the perfect metal to which all others are gradually transmuted as they lie in the earth. The object of alchemy is to accelerate this process and arrive at perfection by man-made means. But Subtle perverts this desire for absolute perfection, which man has in common with Nature, to the desire for relative or earthly perfection—for perfect power, perfect wealth, perfect pleasure. He dedicates himself, like Ovid, to the use of what should be spiritually directed processes for physically directed purposes. He is no aspiring philosopher, but a conspiring charlatan. The worst of his vice is that, more than half believing in the beneficent powers of the elixir he cannot really make, he mocks these powers by holding out false hope of them to deceive his dupes. He is a devotee of alchemy in the same sense in which Don Giovanni is a devotee of love. When Subtle speaks to his associates in language filled with the terms of his art, his words are not, like Face's superficially similar speeches, meant for humorous effect. On the contrary, as Subtle tells Face what Sir Epicure expects to do with the philosopher's stone, he implies that the knight's dreams are not a priori incapable of realization:

> Me thinkes, I see him, entring ordinaries
> Dispensing for the poxe; and plaguy-houses,
> Reaching his dose; walking more-fields for lepers;
> . . .
> And the high-waies, for beggars, to make rich:
> I see no end of his labours. He will make
> Nature asham'd, of her long sleepe: when art
> Who's but a step-dame, shall doe more, then shee,
> In her best love to man-kind, ever could.
> If his dreame last, hee'll turne the age, to gold. (A, I.4.18–29)

The unfortunate feature of the dream is not that it cannot be realized but that the dreamer has come to Subtle for aid in its realization. The dream is the legitimate vision of the beneficent philosopher, and Subtle is

sufficiently rapt with it to speak in the future tense rather than the sub-
junctive of contrary-to-fact conditional. The only conditional, "If his
dream last," is completed by the future tense; even this possibility is not
contrary to fact. Since Subtle knows that the dream will not last, the only
explanation for his hypothetical statement is that he believes in the possibility of its lasting were it not entrusted to him. He knows that there are
essences—that is, essential truths; he knows that Nature does work toward
perfection; but he uses his "art" to pervert this knowledge. It is here that
he resembles the perverted artist Don Giovanni, whose masterly imitation
of love, based on knowledge of its genuine existence, lures his dupes to
their ruin for his profit.

Subtle is unlike the Don, however, in that the Alchemist's victims are
not seduced: like Volpone's gulls, they are already self-deceived. They are
all looking for short cuts through or paths around their natural lot. The
vice of Subtle and the folly of his dupes are the same: impiety against the
force that rules the world. They will not be content with the natural
sequence of events. They must have "the secret/ Of nature, naturiz'd"
(II.1.63–64): the quintessence of Nature; "the art of *Angels,* Natures
miracle,/ The *divine secret*" (III.2.103–04)—everything that man cannot
possess and dare not attempt to control, they want for their personal and
private use. They are like Volpone's would-be heirs in desiring immoral
impossibilities from that mystical "oyle," the elixir; but they exceed
their counterparts, as Subtle exceeds Volpone himself, in the blasphemy
of seeking as "oyle" no man-made artificial substance, but the perfection
Nature creates for a different, a truthful and beneficent, end. Subtle undertakes not to aid Nature, an assistance which is the prerogative and duty of
the true artist, but to "teach dull nature/ What her owne forces are"
(IV.1.88–89).

This is also what he teaches the dull dupes. He does not seduce them,
he merely shows them what are the inner forces that motivate their action,
and encourages further action on the same motivation. When Sir Epicure
in his scene with Dol praises as signs of noble blood her Valois nose, her
Medici forehead, her Austriac lip and chin, he is prompted by no one; he
is self-gulled by his desires. Like Dapper in the privy, like Drugger in his
tobacco shop, he *will* believe what the Alchemist has shown him he

wants to believe. That is the trick of Subtle's "philosopher's stone": it
changes nothing; it merely acts as a touchstone. Men can be transmuted by
it as little as metals. Surly, the only character not taken in by the schemers,
is shocked at the quality he recognizes in the stone:

> Hart! can it be,
> That a grave sir, a rich, that has no need,
> A wise sir, too, at other times, should thus
> With his owne oathes, and arguments, make hard meanes
> To gull himselfe? And this be your *elixir,*
> Your *lapis mineralis,* and your *lunarie,*
> Give me your honest trick, yet, at *primero.* (II.3.278–84)

He prefers to see one man cheated by another rather than by himself. It is a
sight not merely ludicrous but painful to watch a man's driving force become his vanity, his small (as in the case of Dapper) hopes or smaller (as
in the case of Drugger) dreams—which might have remained decently
hidden but for the alchemy of Face, Subtle, and Dol. "In vain," says the
Herford and Simpson introduction to *The Alchemist,* "Paracelsus vindi-
cated the 'divine science' of alchemy, which has but one end—to extract
the quintessence of things—against the 'false disciples' who took its end to
be the making of gold and silver."[27] He would not have had to vindicate it
against the trinity in Lovewit's house; they practiced the true science.

Subtle is aware of this aspect of his work. He declares that he has
"wrought" Face "to *quintessence*" (I.1.70) from a state in which he "had
no name" (I.1.81); that is, he has taught Face what his own forces are: the
ability to change character at a moment's notice and out-Face all opponents. But Subtle, like Morose and Volpone, destroys the little world
within which he is successful. Like Morose when he introduces Epicoene
into his house, like Volpone when he introduces Celia into his, Subtle
contradicts his own handiwork by attempting to outface Face; like
Morose and Volpone, he oversteps the boundaries of his handiwork when
he attempts to extend his deception to Lovewit, who owns the house and
is thus outside and above it.

27. HS, 2, 92.

All three are overcome by their own constructions. Morose, attempting to live an artificial life, finds that he has succeeded too well: in his world everything turns artificial, even his wife, that artificially silent artificial woman. Volpone, attempting to live a life of total deceit, finds that in his world everything turns to deceit; he himself has determined Mosca's falsehood, for there cannot be an honest man in a world such as he has constructed. In Subtle's world everything turns to its quintessence; Face, true to the essence Subtle has shown him, changes character immediately upon his master's reappearance and takes Lovewit's side against his former colleagues. Ironically enough, this final change of character involves a return to the essence Subtle originally recognized in him: he becomes once more Lovewit's impecunious and dependent butler. More than ironically enough, each of the three rulers of an artificial world is ruined by his continued belief in precisely that which he has devoted his life to ridiculing or denying: Volpone by his trust in human affection and loyalty, Morose by his reliance on natural traits, Subtle by his confidence in the efficacy of transformation. Each is outwitted by Nature, using exactly the means by which he has attempted to outwit her. Subtle's final attempt at alchemy, the transmutation of Face into a dupe, is unsuccessful; the artist, even the artist of deceit, succeeds only so long as he works with, not against, Nature —in this case human nature. Face's essential nature Subtle has been able to bring out; he cannot undo his own work. The last step of his Herculean attempt succeeds only too well: he cleanses himself and Dol out of Lovewit's house.

Society, however, is not cleansed. Subtle and Dol are still abroad, and one feels certain that they will find some other house in which to set up shop. Their dupes, to be sure, are discomfited, but so are their opponents. Surly is outwitted in his attempt to marry one of their intended victims; Lovewit, who countenances the deceit, gets her instead. Again because of Lovewit, the law is foiled in its attempt to deal with the offenders—a situation unprecedented and unrepeated in Jonson. Neither the honesty in an individual nor the honesty in society avails against fraud in *The Alchemist*. But then, the honesty of the individual concerned is not entirely altruistic: Surly's rescue of Dame Pliant from a fate worse than death carries the taint of self-interest, unlike Bonario's rescue of Celia. As for the honesty of society, it resides entirely in those who symbolize it: the police. Since these guardians of true morality have in this play no true morality to guard, their attempts must fail. The moral disease of Face, Subtle, and Dol is everywhere, encouraged by the tolerance of the intelligent and the helplessness of the foolish. The dupes represent a larger cross section of society than in any other play. In contrast to the scoundrels of all the others, the fraudulent trio takes up residence not in a house of their own but in the house of a representative of society. The implication is that vice and perversion are possible because of society's moral equivocation and eye to the main chance. Lovewit's moral failings provide a point to which actual vices can attach themselves as servants. The master allows himself to be practiced upon and practices upon others, while the only other visible members of society, the neighbors, stand by, too foolish to do anything at all. Active and passive encouragement of vice permit it a lasting place in the world: the achievements of the artificial microcosm are integrated all too well into the unnatural microcosm of the play's world.

The Alchemist, then, presents a society in which men are either incapable of judgment or unwilling to exercise it. This play with its structure of "base metal" reveals an acceptance of evil unusual but not unparalleled in Jonson:

> no wonder if the world, growing old, begin to be infirme: Old age it selfe is a disease. It is long since the sick world began to doate, and talke idly: Would she had but doated still; but her dotage is now broke forth into a madnesse, and become a meere phrency. *(D, 301–05)*

The Alchemist is the only play in which the phrency is allowed to escape beyond the walls of its asylum. But even here a careful distinction is drawn between society and Nature: the latter works, as always, to reveal and destroy vice, but the former will not take advantage of the world's inherent truthfulness. For "I cannot thinke *Nature* is so spent, and decay'd, that she can bring forth nothing worth her former yeares. She is alwayes the same, like her selfe: . . . Men are decay'd . . . Shee is not" *(D, 124–28).*

Nature is forever equally perfect. The little world which opposes hers is always the creation of a decadent man, never of a poet-figure, for Jonson does not view art as man's refuge against Nature. On the contrary, it is only by complete acceptance of Nature that man can avoid annihilation by her; as her opponent, he has no chance. That is why those psychological fortresses against human nature, the Humors, inner versions of the artificial microcosm, must be destroyed before man can take his place in society. The attempt to preserve and emphasize one's identity forcibly in the face of chaos and flux may be, psychologically speaking, a natural impulse, but it is, metaphysically speaking, futile. The only right, the only successful, answer is to seek, to understand, and finally to accept the laws which underlie apparent chaos itself, to build in accordance with these laws the one kind of society which can last. It is only Jonson's villains, never his heroes, who are irregularly great. The ideal individual is a public man, integrated into a valid pattern, the pattern enriched by his inclusion. He applies to society's salvation man's best intellectual and spiritual qualities: clemency, manliness, critical judgment, poetic understanding. These are the qualities Jonson brings to bear upon his creations and his creatures for the benefit of his society, in his capacity as its public man.

The action of Jonson's plays, then, recapitulates the action of his ideal poet. Even when there is no true artist within the play to take over, with respect to its unenlightened characters, the same duties Jonson conceives himself to have with respect to his unenlightened audience, the pattern of the play itself brings enlightenment to its characters and thus acts out, as it were, the poet's task. Inevitably, Jonson's view of the poet's role circumscribes his material. Chaos, madness, and uncontrolled passion can appear only as mistakes, as the corrigible precursors of stability— or at least of the clear revelation which makes stability possible. They are the enemies of pattern, substituting personal desire for general desirability.

Jonson has had much to bear from critics irresistibly tempted to set him against his greatest contemporary, unequaled expositor of the private man. Apart from date, however, there is very little similarity in the intention or achievements of their work to make such comparisons fruitful. Jonson's plays are about moral judgment. Since that is their concern, the God's plenty that is evident in Shakespeare's world and characters, exact moral judgment on which is seldom possible or desirable, is not only irrelevant to Jonson's purpose but would actually undermine it. He is presenting the moral essence of the universe, not a reflection of its apparently chaotic functioning. The motive behind his comedy as well as his tragedy is the impulse to impart what he has seen, both in the marvelously symmetrical realm of the spirit and the frighteningly deformed realm of the flesh. The microcosmic mirror that is his work shows on one half its spherical surface a distorted picture of the world he inhabits, a picture in which those figures nearest the center are most misshapen; viewed through the other hemisphere, the mirror proves to be half-silvered and grants a clear view into the true world of the poet's vision. The world of Jonson's plays is multifarious but schematized, for he is revealing the scheme of the world.

Being a poet's poet, he is perhaps in all ages best understood and judged according to criteria formulated by the artist, in assertions about his craft inspired by a conviction whose sources are, after all, not available to the critic:

> But the top pleasure consists in having hit the sense or taste of reality, in having been able, in having succeeded in rendering the *atmosphere of being,* the surrounding whole, the total environment, the frame, where the particular and depicted thing is . . . plunged and floating.

> When from the fabric . . . we gradually, one after another, subtract characters, their development, situations, occurrences, the plot, the subject, the content . . . The second-rate diverting literature will leave no remainder after such a subtraction. But the [greatest] creation . . . lets remain the *cardinal:* the characterisation of reality as such; almost as of a philosophic category; as a member or link of our minds' universe; as life's perpetual companion and surroundings.[28]

28. Boris Pasternak, letter of 22 August 1959 to Stephen Spender, in "B. Pasternak: Three Letters," *Encounter, 15,* No. 2 (1960), 4–5.

3. Clues to Just Judgment: I

Justum judicium judicate.

John 7:24.

He only judges right, who weighs, compares,
And, in the sternest sentence which his voice
Pronounces, ne'er abandons charity.

Wordsworth, *Ecclesiastical Sonnets,* II.1

The "critical sense of life,"[1] which Jonson followed further than
any other impulse or talent, led him to pass judgment upon the company
on stage as well as that in the pit; but his main object was to equip the
men and women within the circle of his theater to judge of those within
the circle of his play, and then to extend that understanding to the circle
of his readers, the hoped-for purchasers of the 1616 Folio. But how was
Jonson to make certain of securing the audience's understanding, of
transmitting his perception of Truth to the minds of his spectators and
readers? How ensure that the picture he drew would be durable, lastingly
comprehensible? The latest poet's poet to assess him finds Jonson solv-
ing the problem of communication by placing his meanings where they
would most readily be available, on the "surface" of his poetry, which
appeals to the intellect. If he has lacked sympathetic readers, it is because
they have been unwilling to do the brainwork involved in analyzing
what has been so deliberately placed. In short, T. S. Eliot considers
Ben Jonson a poet not evocative but declarative. He grants that "there

1. Rhys, *Ben Jonson,* p. 26.

are possibilities for Jonson even now . . . but his poetry is of the surface
. . . the polished veneer of Jonson only reflects the lazy reader's fatuity;
unconscious does not respond to unconscious; no swarms of inarticulate
feelings are aroused."[2]

Perhaps the surface has worn so well because it has been so little used.
Even Eliot seems to have been dazzled by the polished veneer he describes
into believing that the effects are all got with mirrors and that we must
think to discover what they really mean. But if Jonson's poetry in his
dramas is poetry of the surface, the surface is likely to be of another kind
than Eliot believes. Aware of the intimate correspondence between
Jonson's theory and practice, one is bound to waver over Eliot's characterization of Jonson's method in the face of Jonson's own censure:
"You have others [wits] that labour onely to ostentation; and are ever
more busie about the colours, and surface of a worke, then in the matter,
and foundation: For that is hid, the other is seene" *(D, 691–94)*.

Jonson's most basic problem was generated precisely by the struggle
between the centrifugal pull of his surfaces and the centripetal pull of
his matter. In this tension lies also the secret of the marvelous balance his
work attains. He felt that he had to express the invisible through the
visible, communicate the ineffable to the eyes and ears of the beholders,
in order to fulfill the poet's double duty as Seer and public man. While his
language, his plots, the action of the characters on the stage, all move
outward from their center to the senses of the audience, the nature of
Jonson's material demands that its expression draw men's minds toward
the ethical center.

Jonson's preoccupation with language as the reflection of man's mind
and as the greatest bond between men is everywhere evident in his
work; his conviction that "*Speech* is the only benefit man hath to expresse his excellencie of mind above other creatures. It is the Instrument
of *Society*" *(D, 1881–83)* is elaborated not only in his treatment of just
and distempered language in his plays but throughout the critical dicta
of *Discoveries*. Nevertheless, he is to be found, in apparent despite

2. Eliot, *Elizabethan Essays*, pp. 66–67.

of his pronouncements on the supremacy of language as communication, yielding the palm to practitioners of a silent art:

> *Whosoever* loves not *Picture,* is injurious to Truth: and all the wisdom of *Poetry*. Picture . . . doth so enter, and penetrate the inmost affection (being done by an excellent Artificer) as sometimes it orecomes the power of speech, and oratory. *(D, 1522–28)*

The key concept in Jonson's statement is that of "the inmost affection." There is a part of man, emotional and spiritual, which responds intuitively to good art ("being done by an excellent Artificer") and leads man to "wisdom." Just as the poet responds intuitively to the universe in order to see the divine vision, so his auditors, the mass of men, respond intuitively to a work of art in order to receive the artist's transmission of what he has beheld. This alogical faculty of the mind or emotions, this "inmost affection," is the bond between artist and audience, the starting point of all possibility of artistic communication, whether it be through poetry or picture or any other art whatsoever. Through this intuition in himself and in all men the artist is able to mediate between earth and heaven. The poet and the painter share in the same process of communication, rely on the same faculty in themselves and in other men, for

> *Poetry,* and *Picture,* are Arts of a like nature; and both are busie about imitation. It was excellently said of *Plutarch, Poetry* was a speaking Picture, and *Picture* a mute Poesie. For they both invent, faine, and devise many things, and accomodate all they invent to the use, and service of nature . . . They both are borne *Artificers,* not made. Nature is more powerfull in them then study. *(D, 1509–21)*

Poet and painter both depend on their intuitive vision, which no amount of hard work can replace. But the poet's attempt to portray the heavenly design by faining and forming a fable and writing things like the truth *(D, 2353–54)* is not always in itself sufficient. Jonson clearly felt at times, as nearly all poets must have done, that language—at least its logical appeal—gets in the way of communication. Language is not always the tool that liberates form from its stone prison; sometimes it is the unyielding rock itself. The poet's struggle becomes a struggle with words as much as with material or audience; he begins to yearn for the "mute Poesie" that can draw what it sees without dependence upon that intractable medium, logical speech. To overcome the limitations inherent in the ordinary use of language, the poet must "invent, faine, and devise" more things than a fable and its appurtenances. He must find devices for appealing to the alogical faculty in men, for penetrating the inmost affection and ensuring just judgment.

As supernatural revelation is necessary for the poet to behold his vision, so a certain amount of revelation, as opposed to statement, is involved in his transmission of his knowledge. Because he knows, or by the use of his critical faculties can analyze, what has activated his own intuition, he is able by his art to activate the intuition of other men. For "the *Poet* must bee able by nature, and instinct, to powre out the Treasure of his minde" *(D,* 2411–13). His *instinct* is vital to his power— his ability to perceive and convey relationships which are not strictly amenable to logic. He is dealing, after all, with material which is superlogical. There is nothing essentially reasonable about absolute value-judgments based upon an eternal pattern. Since, in the final analysis, the standards by which judgment is made must be accepted as given, as unquestionably true, the task of the moral poet is to cause his audience so to accept them. It is by his use of instinct, his own and his audience's, that he is able to "perswade, and leade men" *(D,* 1030), for his powers, if he is to succeed, must go beyond "his wisdome, in dividing: his subtilty, in arguing." These appeals to reason and conscious judgment will not suffice unless he is able to reinforce them with powers less easily analyzed—unless he can control "with what strength hee doth inspire his Readers; with what sweetnesse hee strokes them: . . . How he doth raigne in mens affections; how invade, and breake in upon them; and makes their minds like the thing he writes" *(D,* 787–93). The suggestion is of an influence subtle and almost insidious—alogical, irresistible —by the exercise of which the poet "leades on, and guides us by the hand to Action, with a ravishing delight, and incredible Sweetnes" *(D,* 2399–2400).

The poet's objectives, then, are to make the thing he writes like the truth, and men's minds like the thing he writes. These goals are his means for fulfilling the responsibility his extraordinary powers thrust upon him. His greatest effort must be directed toward fusing metaphysical and practical truth, toward making each fragment of reality he shows his audience into a shard that mirrors the Real. He must choose among those words and actions which will be acceptable both to him and to his audience because they are "naturally" true, because they could have happened or actually have happened, in order to represent in his work such of them as imply the Natural in a higher sense—that of the order and judgment of Nature. He must be like Mercury, "the President of Language . . . *Deorum hominumq́ interpres*" (D, 1883–84).

Often the devices Jonson uses in his plays to imply a higher truth manifest themselves as situations which demand action or reaction from the protagonists. This major technique of Jonson's is well illustrated in the use he makes of his characters' attitudes toward amusement (game-playing), toward money, and toward noble birth.

It is remarkable, for example, how often Jonson, usually thought of as the sensible, down-to-earth playwright in the ranks of the fanciful Elizabethans and Jacobeans, uses the romantic device of resolving a tangled plot by revealing a disguised noble friend or relative to his protagonists. He begins by doing this in *The Case Is Altered,* and he is still doing it in his last two comedies, *The New Inn* and *The Magnetic Lady.* Indeed, the device provides a perfect expression for his conviction that inner truth speaks to inner understanding. Nobility, though issuing in worthy action when called into play, may exist as invisible potentiality, but to the intuition it is visible. Those who apprehend it in Jonson's plays find it out not through any data provided by their observation but through an instinctive response independent of evidence: "if wee will looke with our understanding, and not our senses, wee may behold vertue, and beauty (though cover'd with rags) in their brightnesse" (D, 1429–32).

Thus Rachel (CA), supposed a beggar's daughter, radiates a nobility which dazzles her more perceptive lovers. Paulo, overcome by a conviction of her gentility which he cannot support, concludes that "in difference of good,/ Tis more to shine in vertue then in bloud" (CA,

I.10.37–38). Rachel has up to this point displayed no positive goodness
beyond the capacity to love Paulo, but a lover may be excused for considering this a virtue. His father finds himself similarly moved, and
marvels:

> Tis strange (she being so poore) he should affect her,
> But this is more strange that my selfe should love her.
> I spide her, lately, at her fathers doore,
> And if I did not see in her sweet face
> Gentry and noblenesse, nere trust me more. (II.6.35–39)

Rachel proves in fact to be the long-lost daughter of the Lord Chamount,
justifying by her birth her admirers' intuitive opinion of her. She herself
is unaware of her descent, so that she cannot be acting in accordance
with what she knows is her rightful station. Nobility is simply inherent in
her, as it is in Camillo Ferneze, who is supposed to be the quite ordinary
—not to say common—Frenchman Gasper, a supposition shared by
himself. He carries the tokens of his birth about him in an indefinable
aura; his sister, despite her dedication to chastity, feels an unwonted and,
to her, incomprehensible affection for the supposed Frenchman, even
when he is discovered to have deceived the family by pretending to be
Chamount:

> Something there is in him,
> That doth enforce this strange affection,
> With more then common rapture in my breast:
> For being but *Gasper,* he is still as deare
> To me, as when he did *Chamount* appeare. (IV.11.58–62)

The fact of the matter is that he is dear to her neither because he is
Chamount nor because he is Gasper but because he is her noble brother.
She is the more serious and more seriously affectionate of his two sisters,
therefore more likely to perceive emanations of nobility and fraternal
relationship. Her intuitions are reinforced by those of Camillo's closest
friend, Chamount: "Sure thou art nobly borne,/ How ever fortune hath
obscurd thy birth:/ For native honour sparkles in thine eyes" (IV.4.20–

22). Like Rachel's lovers, Camillo's admirers look with the understanding and behold the truth. The eye and ear may be deceived, but the unaided understanding is incorruptible. Or rather, it is corrupted only in those who are already spiritually corrupt, and it may err in those whose spirit temporarily errs.

The ability to recognize unblazoned nobility becomes a test for virtue in the characters and a device for ensuring the audience's agreement with the playwright. No spectator, except one bent upon being refractory or spitefully refusing the smallest sympathy to the author, willingly identifies with a discredited character. If the acceptance of Rachel as noble separates the sheep from the goats, no spectator will wish to be classed with the goatish Angelo, who advises his enamored friend: "She is derivd too meanely to be wife/ To such a noble person, in my judgement," or to subject himself to Paulo's rebuke: "Nay then thy judgement is to meane, I see" (I.10.34–36). Angelo's judgment informs the spectator that here is an unsound understanding, proclaiming an unsound character. The revelation operates in two ways: the audience receives support for its opinion of Angelo, and is maneuvered into support of the poet's opinion of Rachel, although the girl herself exhibits no more than plaster-of-Paris virtue to support her lover's claims. The statements about her, not her own actions, must carry the day in the minds of the spectators. Further, because the intuition of worthy characters is proved to be infallible, the audience transfers this proof to apply to its own intuition, which has agreed with that upheld by the outcome of the play. Therefore a proposition not only about Rachel but about the infallibility of intuition is impressed upon the minds of the audience.[3]

The process is similar in regard to Camillo. His sister's and Chamount's statements are acceptable to the audience because of the characters who utter them. Through identification with these persons, the spectators come to feel that their own intuition has been activated, that they

3. My assertions, here and elsewhere, as to what the audience feels are, of course, subjective. But the assumption that Jonson's devices work, which must be made if one is to examine their significance, is, after all, a subjective assumption, and the way in which such devices do work can only be analyzed by investigating some extension of a subjective response.

themselves perceive something extraordinary about Camillo. In this way they are prepared for the denouement, which would otherwise seem totally arbitrary but now seems totally true. They perceive that, although their information has been misleading, their understanding has been accurate—another victory for instinct. Meanwhile, Count Ferneze, whose fury at being deceived by "Gasper" has so overcome his better nature as to disable his instinct temporarily, has almost killed his unknown son; but just as his error in outward judgment and honor is made plain by the temporary failure of his inner understanding, so the basic soundness of his character is attested to when his intuition, accurate enough with regard to Rachel, asserts itself the moment he raises his hand against his son:

> Ile heare no more, I say he shall not live,
> My selfe will do it. Stay, what forme is this
> Stands betwixt him and me, and holds my hand?
> What miracle is this? tis my owne fancy,
> Carves this impression in me, my soft nature,
> . . .
>   . . . What a child am I
> To have a child? Ay me, my son, my son. (V.9.21–29)

Despite his firm intentions, despite his reason, despite his emotions, Ferneze's "inmost affection" takes over and guides him by the hand to Action, with incredible sweetness. Ferneze yields to the truth set up by Nature, and the audience yields to the truth set up by the poet.

When a character is unable to perceive the truth determined by Nature, poet and audience reject the dullard, for to be dull of inner vision is criminal stupidity, rendering men unfit for divine revelation. It is a total condemnation of Saviolina *(EO)* and the court life she represents that her intuition of nobility does not function, and the entire scene that discredits her and her way of life turns upon this failure. Confident that she can distinguish a nobleman from a country clown, she is presented by Macilente and his cohorts with a veritable clown upon whom to try her perspicacity, and falls—or rather, casts herself headlong—into the trap:

> they were verie bleare-witted, yfaith, that could not discerne the
> gentleman in him . . . why, if you had any true court-judgement in
> the carriage of his eye, and that inward power that formes his
> countenance, you might perceive his counterfeiting as cleere, as the
> noone-day: . . . Why, gallants, let me laugh at you, a little: was this
> your device, to trie my judgement in a gentleman?
>
> $\qquad\qquad\qquad\qquad\qquad\qquad\qquad\qquad$ *(EO,* V.2.73–79, 102–03)

It was not so much the gallants' device as the playwright's: in trying her judgment in a gentleman, he tries her judgment in all matters to be grasped by inner understanding. Since her failure and humiliation reflect not only upon her but upon all those who accept her standards of "court-judgement," the audience must reject her false colors and take up the standard of the poet. He has made it plain to the spectators—more plain than he could have done by any rhymed soliloquy on the subject—that the substitution of outer for inner criteria or values is a sign of corruption.

The implications of Jonson's exempla extend beyond their effects upon fellow characters and audience to form a concept of nobility itself. While many of his characters' statements, like those given to Paulo, seem to express a euphuistic view which "makes gentility a matter of the individual man,"[4] by a curious coincidence the individual man in question always turns out to be nobly born and the possessor of large amounts of money. The ultimate justification of intuition proves to be outer circumstance. But this is the curious coincidence of inner and outer reality upon which Jonson always insists; it by no means vitiates what he has to say about spiritual qualities. On the contrary, it confirms the assurance that the material world shapes itself around the spiritual, that

4. Baskervill, *English Elements,* p. 142. For a discussion of sources for conflicting ideals of nobility in the English Renaissance, see Baskervill, pp. 141–42. For a more detailed account of the conflict between individual integrity and high birth as criteria, see Lewis Einstein, *The Italian Renaissance in England* (New York, 1902), pp. 61ff.

form and content are, under ideal circumstances, at one. While nobility does not derive from high birth or riches, these are its proper manifestations and they will, when error is done away with, be found making innate gentility visible to the public eye. They are the practical truth through which a metaphysical truth manifests itself, the practical truth which can stand, for the audience, as symbol of the metaphysical.

Before error has been done away with, nobility may, in exceptional cases, be a matter not of actual though disguised position but of unregarded desert. The two grand exceptions who prove Jonson's rule of birth are Crites and Cicero, who are both explicitly said to be entitled to ruling positions in their respective commonwealths and to prosperity, although Cicero must wait for the election and Crites for the end of the play to receive appropriate social status. Here attitude is more important than fact; Jonson makes it clear at every turn that to deny social position to these two is to keep them from their rights. Nature has ordained them for nobility, and the fact that her prophecy remains unfulfilled is a result of the corrupt behavior of men.

This view, considerably more complex than the doctrine usually ascribed to Jonson, of nobility through good works, informs his dramas from first to last. As so often, he is to be found squarely on the side of predestination: men are born for nobility or not. If they are born for nobility in preeminent virtue, they are born for nobility in preeminent position. Nature is even-handed, and Nature's world is perfect; no one can deserve worldly nobility to whom she does not give it: that would be a flaw in the construction of the universe. If an innkeeper's manner of speech makes him appear to "talke above your seasoning,/ Ore what you seem" (NI, I.3.89–90), if his guests "easily suspect" that he was born to a place above his present and see him "confesse it,/ Both i'your language, treaty, and your bearing" (I.3.96–99), then it is better than a thousand to one that that innkeeper will prove to be no innkeeper, but a Lord. The discredit of the disguise, if there be any, will lie not with the harmless deceiver but with those so harmed in understanding as to be deceived: "But if I be no such; who then's the Rogue,/ In understanding, Sir, I meane? who erres?" (I.3.118–19). Those who cannot see, within the lowly Light Heart, its owner's noble light heart are ridiculous and culpable, for "Truth lyes open to all" *(D,* 139–40), if we can but read the page which is uppermost. There are in Jonson no mute inglorious noblemen: if they are noble, they will show it and someone will recognize it; if it cannot be seen, it is not there. Even in his concept of the ideal or metaphysical universe, Jonson was not apt to multiply entities unnecessarily; his gentle men and gentlemen were one and the same.

Jonson's metaphysical universe cannot be improved; it can only degenerate. Human beings may corrupt what Nature has made perfect: a man nobly born may yield to vice, deforming his spirit till it no longer fits the mold in which it was cast. The foolish Saviolina and the affected and semi-immoral Fastidius Briske (he is half-engaged in a half-liaison with his banker's wife) are the fringes of such corruption in society; they are highly born and placed, though not actually noble, and serve as examples to the simpler citizens beneath them. Woven more closely into the fabric of society are the courtiers of Gargaphie. They should present a pattern for the mass of men, who are not favored with access to that potentially perfect microcosm, the court, but instead they "bring the name of courtier in contempt" *(CR,* V.i.36). While a foolish citizen corrupts only himself, and a minor member of the gentry corrupts those who see and emulate him, as Fungoso does Fastidius Briske, court functionaries are responsible for the well-being of an entire society: "A vertuous *Court* a world to vertue drawes" *(CR,* V.11.173).

Perfectly central to the pattern of society stands the figure of its ruler and representative; if that is corrupt, the whole society is diseased. This is the case in *Catiline* and *Sejanus;* that part of the Roman world which allows itself to be represented by Catiline or Tiberius is, like its figurehead, rotten through and through:

> "Princes, that would their people should doe well,
> "Must at themselves begin, as at the head;
> "For men, by their example, patterne out
> "Their imitations, and reguard of lawes. *(CR,* V.11.169–72)

In his struggle with Cicero, first for the position of consul, then for control of the state, Catiline rules only a faction; decay can be cut out of the state with the cutting-out of this its source. But in Tiberius' Rome the imitation which is patterned out has become a diabolical rather than a heavenly design. In this state the rot has spread too far to be eliminated: limbs may be severed to restore a tree to health, but the roots never. The distance of corrupt nobility from the center of society provides an accurate unit of measurement for the extent of that society's decay. It is proper that such measurement should prove accurate, for corruption of nobility indicates decay of that divine pattern which equates inner and outer preeminence.

Since nobility of birth may be perverted, it cannot be taken as a necessarily true sign of inner worth. We must look to behavior, manner, bearing; then our judgment will be substantiated, not determined, by outer adornments. If the only true signs of gentility are noble action and demeanor, it is merely a step (logically fallacious but dramatically convincing) to the proposition that noble action and demeanor are signs only of true gentility: *"The vulgar* are commonly ill-natur'd" *(D,* 972). The well-natur'd gentlefolk in disguise are easily spotted through rags and apparent low connections; they must be well born, for they are well behaved.

Yet in a deeper sense, action and demeanor, too, are appurtenances; they are the manifestations of nobility, not nobility itself. Nobility is an inherent, not-quite-definable component of the best natures, an essence. Jonson tended to think in terms of essences, to which he then assigned—or for which he observed—varied outer manifestations, and his view of gentility conforms to this tendency, granting essential nobility one manifestation not dependent upon high birth: poetic ability. The equation he sets up between exalted lines and exalted lineage is not so eccentric as it may at first seem: both are gifts of nature unattainable through human effort, both place their possessors among a minority of outstanding men in their society, and both provide means for those who have them to offer those who do not an understanding of a portion of the divine pattern. True nobility is the moral aspect of the truly poetic spirit—that impulse in man which strives toward the highest good.

Crites and Cicero, then, combine in themselves the moral and aesthetic forms of that impulse; embodying both the good man and the good artist, they are universally recognized to be supreme in talent and instinctively recognized as supreme in nobility. Cicero, a passer-by unknown to the ambassadors of the Allobroges at Rome, strikes "an awe" *(C,* IV.45) into them: "How easie is a noble spirit discern'd" (IV.50), they remark with admiration but without surprise. His bearing alone convinces them that he is fit for high position, impressing them with

> a more reguard
> Unto his place, then all the boystrous moodes
> That ignorant greatnesse practiseth, to fill
> The large, unfit authoritie it weares. (IV.46–49)

Indeed, Cicero is explicitly set forth as the man of low birth and noble nature who confronts and overcomes the man of low nature and noble birth. His eloquence testifies to the elevation of his spirit, which is resented by Sempronia, adherent of the corrupt old order:

> Hang vertue, where there is no bloud: 'tis vice,
> And, in him, sawcinesse. Why should he presume
> To be more learned, or more eloquent,
> Then the nobilitie? (II.122–25)

Even she is forced to grant him "qualitie/ Worthy a noble man, himselfe not noble" (II.125–26), but her sympathies force her to assert that his qualities are not what they are—that although he is noble, he is not noble. The fact that her position is necessarily self-contradictory annihilates her argument and supports Jonson's: a man in whom love and aptitude for virtue have reached such a point that they express themselves as sublime eloquence is a man naturally noble. Cicero is juxtaposed against the decay of the ancient pattern as an incarnation of that pattern freshly reinstated: " 'Twas vertue onely, at first, made all men noble" (II.127), Sempronia is reminded, and she replies: "I yeeld you, it might, at first, in Romes poore age;/ When both her Kings, and *Consuls* held the plough,/ Or garden'd well" (II.128–30). What she does not realize is that the cycle is beginning again, this time in the garden of eloquence: *magnus ab integro saeclorum nascitur ordo.*

Ennoblement through artistic power is the fortune also of Crites, whose worth is known, although his height's untaken. He is an aspirant

toward goodness, indeed toward divinity, so "studious of deserving well"
that he is "(to speake truth) indeed deserving well" (CR, V.6.85, 86).
As already observed, nobility leads to noble action when the opportunity
arises, but it is recognizable by the perceptive even before it is manifested.
Thus Cynthia is able to say of Crites, before she has been introduced to
him or seen his masque,

> We have alreadie judg'd him, ARETE:
> Nor are we ignorant, how noble minds
> Suffer too much through those indignities,
> Which times, and vicious persons cast on them. (V.6.101–04)

Nobility needs no formal introduction; worthy natures recognize it as an
old friend before it speaks its name:

> "Potentiall merit stands for actuall,
> "Where onely oportunitie doth want,
> "Not will, nor power: both which in him abound. (V.6.87–89)

To what extent Ben Jonson's sense of his own position influenced his
theory is a matter for psychological speculation rather than critical analysis. His own utterances suffice to show how he was galled by the spurs
of ambition in a society which had not the slightest intention of elevating
its moral artist to a position beside its ruler. The status of the bricklayer-
turned-poet was so far removed from the social nobility to which he
nonetheless felt certain claims (as testified to in his conversations with
Drummond [234–36]) that a view of nobility as innate, though properly
decked in the splendor and authority his own decayed society denied him,
seems the only congenial construction he could have put upon his situation. Perhaps he made up to his fictional colleagues Cicero and Crites and
even Virgil the injuries he felt he had received.

The concept of innate nobility is more interesting, however, for its
philosophical than for its psychological implications. We have seen
Jonson upholding an inspirational theory of poetry; now we find him
championing a concomitant intuitive theory of ethics. Noble ancestors
and training in virtue do not ensure nobility in the offspring who are
products of this ultrafavorable environment and heredity. The only

assurance of virtue lies in an instinctive perception of it, common in its highest form to the poet and the man of truly noble spirit. These two sorts of men can unerringly judge the quality of human actions and the quality of poetry, since their preternaturally clear vision enables them to compare both with their divine original. Thus Mercury assures Crites, uncertain of the reception of his work, that

> The better race in court
> That have the true nobilitie, call'd vertue,
> Will apprehend it, as a gratefull right
> Done to their separate merit. *(CR,* V.i.30–33)

Jonson's epistemology, in short, is entirely intuitive; ethics and aesthetics are double aspects of a single perception of the Good. The instinct that enables a man to recognize a good action is the same that enables him to recognize a good work of art. The flow of intuition divides from its single source into two streams, which merge again in the timeless ocean of undifferentiated Good. One stream carries men toward acknowledgment of a human being fashioned in the image of God, the other toward acknowledgment of a work fashioned in the image of the divine pattern. Such acknowledgment is effortless for the truly good man, impossible for the truly depraved; it is to be achieved through proper stimulus, proper exertion, by the mass of men, whose goodness is obscured but not corrupted, for "good men, like the sea,/ should still maintaine/ Their noble taste, in midst of all fresh humours,/ That flow about them, to corrupt their streames" *(CR,* V.i.13–15).

Jonson, then, utilizes his spectators' artistic perception to lead them on to moral judgment. When he employs a device that goes beyond logic, he avails himself of the poet's legitimate means to establish a standard that goes beyond logic. Such stimulus to the audience's moral intuition is provided by one of his most cherished symbols—money, which, the more it is used, the brighter it grows, illuminating in turn the condition of purses, persons, and perceptions.

Everybody in Jonson likes money. Some characters are not in want of it, others do not particularly want it, but nobody is actually averse to it, and the consensus of characters is distinctly in favor. No valid discussion of money as a symbol in Jonson is possible unless one begins by discarding the assumption that "gold must be condemned as a positive danger, not a neutral substance misapplied in the hands of its possessors."[5] A neutral substance, sometimes misapplied, is precisely what it is—a better-than-neutral substance, in fact, and, like nobility, a legitimate outer expression of inner value, to which worthy men are entitled and unworthy men are not. There is no reason why a good solid man should not possess good solid coin. Jonson liked it himself, and some of his best characters take after him. Sir Dauphine Eugenie is on the track of "a steady income and an inheritance";[6] Lady Loadstone most desires for her niece full payment of the girl's dowry; Wittipol and Manly consider the saving of Fitz-Dottrell's fortune of equal importance with the saving of his wife; the Host sees to it that his daughter's maid Prudence, witty mistress of the revels at the sign of the Light Heart, receives "a just portion" (NI, V.5.133) toward her marriage; Celia, in compensation for her husband's and the court's ill-treatment, is sent home to her father "with her dowrie trebled" (V, V.12.144); and Peniboy Junior's father turns out to be a walking encomium on wealth justly used (SN). Even Virgil has his Maecenas, and Crites his Cynthia, whose assurance that "CYNTHIA shall brighten, what the world made dimme" (CR, V.6.3) affords good hope of a competency.

Money may indeed be the golden means to a good life. Volturtius, the renegade conspirator who ends by informing against Catiline, would in Caesar's opinion be amply rewarded by a grant of "life, and favour"; but Cato, wisest of Romans, overrides the erstwhile culprit's "I aske no more" with a vehement assertion: "Yes, yes, some money, thou need'st it./ 'Twill keepe thee honest: want made thee a knave" (C, V.298–300).

5. Enck, Comic Truth, p. 121. Enck is referring to the gold in Volpone, but even in this play Celia's trebled dowry counts against him. The widely accepted view of Jonson as opponent of all forms of materialism, and particularly of money itself, can be traced in large part to L. C. Knights' classic statement of this position in Drama and Society in the Age of Jonson (London, 1937).

6. Jonas A. Barish, Ben Jonson and the Language of Prose Comedy (Cambridge, Mass., 1960), p. 185.

It is unreasonable and unwise to expect a man of ordinary spirit to get on without a modicum of money; one might as well expect him to bear himself with dignity without any clothes on. Only a man of extraordinary sensibilities and an exceptional sense of innate merit would be able to overcome or ignore the public disadvantages attendant upon either sort of bareness. A reasonable amount of money, like a sober suit of clothes, contributes to a man's sense of himself and enables him to uphold the dignity of man by being able to exhibit its outward signs. Jonson himself agrees with Cato: "*I have seene*, that *Poverty* makes men doe unfit things; but honest men should not doe them: they should gaine otherwise" (*D*, 1070–72). He does not say they should not gain: money will support their honesty as their honesty supports them.

On the other hand, for a man like Sir Epicure Mammon money obviates the necessity for clothes. Gilded with the elixir which represents untold wealth, he will parade his nudity before

> my glasses,
> Cut in more subtill angles, to disperse,
> And multiply the figures, as I walke
> Naked betweene my *succubae*. (*A*, II.2.45–48)

His sensual nakedness is to him a source of glory; he does not recognize it as naked sensuality. Without waiting for the advent of the satirist, he strips his own follies naked as at their birth (*EO*, "*After the Second Sounding*," 17–18), enabled by a golden mirror to "turn shewn nakednesse to impudence" (*CR*, V.4.628). Too much money indicates an inflated sense of personal worth, ballooning so far beyond the sphere proper to the dignity of man that it bursts. Superfluity is the obverse and counterpart of insufficiency: both make men "doe unfit things."

If a man's spirit is to find repose, its resting place should be neither too hard nor too soft. A pallet will not suffice, but to endure that is not more harmful than to "have all my beds, blowne up; not stuft:/ Downe is too hard" (*A*, II.2.41–42). The kind of bed on which Sir Epicure lies in imagination—the kind Volpone, lapped in furs, occupies in fact—is necessary to spirits of a restless sickness and morbid hypersensitivity to reality, which furs and down exclude in much the same way as the padded walls designed for that purpose by Morose, who is also a covetous man.

Covetousness in Jonson, whether it manifests itself in a desire to spend or to hoard, is a sign of what the modern psychologist would call overcompensation and involves what Face and Subtle very properly term projection. A material in itself of neutral worth is gilded by the mind with glittering qualities which render its possession a shield for all the dullness of its owner. Whatever spiritual substance man lacks in himself he finds in this material:

> Thou art vertue, fame,
> Honour, and all things else! Who can get thee
> He shall be noble, valiant, honest, wise— *(V, I.1.25–27)*

The golden oyle proffered and accepted by Volpone, the golden elixir Subtle believes in but cannot make, the golden seed Fitz-Dottrell expects to reap from his reclaimed drowned-lands, all are the stuff of false alchemy —no transformation, but substitution of one thing for another. Sufficiency of worldly goods attends spiritual success; superfluity, or the desire for it, waits on spiritual failure. Covetousness is a pretense to success in the realm in which one has failed. Jaques fails to love the only person who loves him, though his abduction of the little girl is a gesture toward the emotion he cannot feel; in place of the daughter who is very possibly his own, he substitutes his money, "my deere child" *(CA,* III.5.16).[7]

---

7. Cf. above, p. 80. The suggestion that Rachel may after all be Jaques' daughter is made by the miser himself:

> his [Chamount's] daughter, being but two years old,
> . . . lov'd me so, that it would leave
> The nurse her selfe, to come into mine armes,
> . . .
> And since her Lady mother that did dye
> In child-bed of her, lov'd me passing well,
> It may be nature fashiond this affection,
> Both in the child and her: but hees ill bred,
> That ransackes tombes, and doth deface the dead.
> I'le therefore say no more: suppose the rest. (II.1.37–47)

Morose, who cannot feel natural affection for his nephew or imagine it as part of a marital relationship, develops an extreme fondness for his wealth, while Fulvia, unmoved by the passion of her lovers, warms to their gifts. Love of money is a sure sign of emotional sterility; eagerness for wealth, the substitute for a spiritual drive. Volpone's devotion to gold is a parody of man's devotion to God; Sir Epicure's proposed Golden Age, a parody of man's vision of the universal good which constitutes universal pleasure; Fitz-Dottrell's ideal of his wife as display piece for his wealth, a parody of man's tendency to cherish an ideal of woman or simply a woman. In every case the overflowing moneybag symbolizes the dried-out soul.

So, inevitably, none of the misers or spendthrifts has any taste at all, any innate nobility or sense of poetry except what is corrupted, or any ability to perceive the good in life or in art (consider Volpone's delight with the doggerel and clowning of his three deformed slaves): the spiritually worthwhile is hidden from them by a golden curtain which they themselves have drawn. Once it has fallen into place, they can turn the other way and play to their audience with the curtain as backdrop, convinced that it will dazzle the spectators, unaware that for those of just vision it will illuminate the actors' true features. For covetousness is not only a means to self-deception; it is an attempt to deceive. Inner poverty is to be masked from other men, as well as from oneself, by a golden visor.

The donning of the visor, the drawing of the curtain, are no passive yieldings to circumstance or surrender to corruption; they are actions requiring positive effort. Covetousness goes beyond debasement of noble birth as a symbol for man's distortion of the heavenly order. The covetous man has not lost the pattern; he has flung it from him with both hands. The curtain he has hung up hides from him the eternal design; the visor he has assumed hides the earthly design of society. All his effort is directed inward, to fill an unfillable void—unfillable because material objects cannot deaden the cavernous echoes of spiritual emptiness. So obsessed is he with his futile attempt to fill his very real needs that he has no concern, no energy to spare, for the order of God or the order of society—the two designs travestied by those most striking of Jonson's getters and spenders, Volpone and Sir Epicure Mammon, the figures most clearly expressive of Jonson's intentions in portraying greed.

Sir Epicure is the more interestingly complex of these two. Less emblematic and more human (perhaps because he does not have to bear the stress of standing at dead center of the wheel's revolution), he is capable of undergoing degenerative development and even reaching despair of sorts: "I will goe mount a turnep-cart, and preach/ The end o'the world, within these two months" (*A*, V.5.81–82). Only by virtue of the turnip cart does Jonson at this moment maintain the comic framework out of which despair speaks. Sir Epicure sees the impossibility of righteous revenge on the three sharpers as the end of the world, because it makes final his position as their moral dupe: he cannot recover his goods unless he publicizes what he has become. Earlier, when he was unaware of his moral bankruptcy (though admitting the manly fault of lust), his financial loss was not of great importance to him; when Subtle's experiment is presumed to have exploded, it is Subtle, not Mammon, who "faints." The end of the world is not the end of financial prospects, which are infinitely renewable, but of that which underlies them in fact and in symbol: the end of self-delusion.

Sir Epicure's particularly ironic self-delusion takes the form of a conviction that he yearns for a figurative Golden Age, whereas in fact he only yearns for a literal one. Unlike the manipulating cynics, he believes in and values generosity, the presence of which he radically overestimates in his own nature: he prides himself on being the opposite of what Volpone prides himself on being. What he asserts to be his object in obtaining the elixir is the outgrowth of a distinctly social consciousness; even Subtle believes that Mammon would be found

> entring ordinaries
> Dispensing for the poxe; and plaguy-houses,
> Reaching his dose; walking more-fields for lepers;
> . . .
> And the high-waies, for beggars, to make rich. (*A*, I.4.18–25)

But the closer he comes to actual possession of the philosopher's stone, the keener grows his sense that charity begins at home. At the beginning of the visit which he expects to crown his hopes, his benevolence has

already contracted to a narrower circle: "This is the day wherein, to all
my friends,/ I shall pronounce the happy word, *be rich*" (II.1.6–7). True,
he still thinks to "undertake, withall, to fright the plague/ Out o' the
kingdome, in three months" (69–70), but his concomitant assertion
that the stone's possessor "by it's vertue,/ Can confer honour, love,
respect, long life,/ Give safety, valure, yea, and victorie,/ To whom he
will" (49–52), exhibits the now impure motivation for his benefactions.
When for the first time Mammon faces the practical worries of a man
of affairs ("Where to get stuffe, inough now, to project on"), social
theory yields without a struggle to material necessity: "FAC. . . . Buy/
The covering of o' churches. MAM. Thats true," and material necessity
breeds thrift: "FAC. . . . cap 'hem, new, with shingles. MAM. No, good
thatch:/ Thatch will lie light upo' the rafters" (II.2.12–17). The lavish-
ness of the original vision is henceforth reserved for benefits accruing to
Mammon himself.

Each further assurance from Face that the work is near completion
provides the impulse for a further defection from the social ideal. When
Mammon's eager "Blushes the *bolts-head?*" (9) receives the desired
answer, the fate of the church roofs crystallizes, but Mammon can still
conceive a gesture of purely personal generosity: *"Lungs,* I will manumit
thee, from the fornace;/ I will restore thee thy complexion, *Puffe,*/ Lost
in the embers; and repaire this braine,/ Hurt wi' the fume o'the mettalls"
(18–21). But with alchemical rapidity this gratitude to a person who has
been of use transforms itself into a hold over his further usefulness, as
recognition of value begets desire to possess:

MAM. Thou hast descryed the *flower,* the *sanguis agni?*

FAC. Yes, sir.

. . .

MAM.   *Lungs,* I will set a period,
To all thy labours: Thou shalt be the master
Of my *seraglia.* (28–33)

The power to free implies the power to imprison. Far now from thinking
in terms of physical restoration, Mammon adds: "But doe you heare?/
I'll geld you, *Lungs*" (34). The power to heal implies the power to

maim. We are now approaching Volpone's moral territory, and these new
stirrings in Mammon demand confirmation: "Th'art sure, thou saw'st it
bloud?" (40). When this transformation from neutral matter (bolt's-
head) to beauty (flower) to violence (blood) is upheld by Face, the power
of blood issues in a burst of lasciviousness and moral sadism ("Both
bloud, and *spirit,* sir" [40]) which obliterates the distinction between
Mammon and Volpone completely:

> Where I spie
> A wealthy citizen, or rich lawyer,
> Have a sublim'd pure wife, unto that fellow
> I'll send a thousand pound, to be my cuckold.
> ...
> ... I'll ha' no bawds,
> But fathers, and mothers. They will doe it best.
> Best of all others. And, my flatterers
> Shall be the pure, and gravest of Divines,
> That I can get for money. My mere fooles,
> Eloquent burgesses, and then my poets,
> The same that writ so subtly of the *fart* ... (53–63)

Mammon has moved from rewarding the oppressed to rewarding
the oppressors. Like Volpone, he now intends to spend his wealth
destroying, not upholding, the qualities and relations on which society
depends. Further, the very concept of society is crumbling: the body
politic is transformed into Mammon's household staff. His dependents
will embody, like the members of Volpone's household, grotesque dis-
tortions of family feeling, of sexual drive, of linguistic force. When
Mammon next asserts a version of his original dream of society, it is as
acknowledged hypocrisy, a ruse to get the elixir, and his language presents a pallid shadow of his original imagination:

> I shall employ it all, in pious uses,
> Founding of colledges, and *grammar* schooles,
> Marrying yong virgins, building hospitalls,
> And now, and then, a church. (II.3.49–52)

It is only fitting that Mammon's household is at last clearly placed not within, but over against, structured society:

DOL. But, in a monarchy, how will this be?
The Prince will soone take notice; and both seize
You, and your *stone:* it being a wealth unfit
For any private subject.

The original motives for the acquisition of the stone—altruism, generosity, beneficence—have now become the threats to its possession. To keep his stone, Mammon must flee from society to a place governed by no social law at all, where he can attend to his own needs without disturbance:

Wee'll therefore goe with all, my girle, and live
In a free state; where we will eate our mullets,
...
And have our cockles, boild in silver shells,
...
                              ... and, with these
Delicate meats, set our selves high for pleasure,
And take us downe againe ...
...
And so enjoy a perpetuitie
Of life, and lust. (IV.i.147–66)

Mammon's progressive parody of a pastoral Golden Age is completed in this materially perfect nonsociety. The man who had thought to "fright the plague out of the kingdom" is frighted out of the kingdom himself. His self-banishment, a change of inner state rather than of outer location, seems to be irrevocable, for he reiterates it in his retirement to "a turnep-cart" when Face's version of his early hopes tears away the last shred of dignity with which Mammon has attempted to cover his disgrace:

LOV. What should they [Mammon's metal goods]
         ha' beene, sir, turn'd into gold all?

MAM.   No.
I cannot tell. It may be they should. What then?

LOV. What a great losse in hope have you sustain'd?

MAM. Not I, the common-wealth has.

FAC.   I, he would ha' built
The citie new; and made a ditch about it
Of silver, should have runne with creame from *Hogsden:*
That, every sunday in *More*-fields, the younkers,
And tits, and tom-boyes should have fed on, *gratis.* (V.5.73–80)

This account of Mammon's intention to gratify appetite penetrates to the essence of his dream, revealing it for the parody it always inherently was.

The greedy man, then, is essentially an antisocietal being, as the depraved noble is not. Tiberius, Saviolina, the courtiers of Gargaphie, all believe in, even work toward, a society—corrupt, but a society nonetheless. Volpone, Sir Epicure, Jaques, Morose, Sir Moath Interest—the whole array of those whose highest good is money—are totally self-involved, intent upon the satisfaction of their own imperative needs, working against the requirements of even the most primitive sort of society.

The symbol of money supplements Jonson's epistemology with a clear concept of how man ceases to know. He denies, as Sir Epicure more and more forcefully denies, the instinct which leads him toward the Good, and substitutes the instincts which lead him toward goods. The spirit is made to serve what should serve it—the body; and with this collapse of internal ordering, external ordering becomes a threat to the new condition. Covetousness, like inability to recognize a noble nature, is a symbol, not a reason, for lack of comprehension of the Good.

But covetousness goes beyond nonrecognition of nobility in representing abandonment of any attempt to reach the ideal, whether philosophically or sociologically. The covetous man is a man totally un-Aristotelian, who neither desires to know nor is a political animal. He has given up the purpose for which he was created and turned himself into an emblem and source of deceit. In substituting outer for inner worth, he is actually misrepresenting himself as a complete man—a crime greater than the simple failure to be one. He is substituting his own pattern for God's.

The pride involved in this action is to be overcome, and the human being saved, only by conformity—through a remnant of instinct—to some aspect of the pattern decreed from above. This remnant of instinct shows itself as a response of affection toward other human beings, and makes a man conform to the pattern of human relationships. This is the earthly equivalent of the heavenly design; no man who does not fit himself into the former can hope to understand the latter.

Thus Peniboy Junior loses his spendthrift and acquisitive drives as soon as filial affection appears to take their place. When his father reveals himself and chastens Peniboy Junior, when the latter is moved to write his sire "a penitent Epistle" (SN, V.1.95), the young man ceases to have any interest in money. He successfully intrigues on behalf of his father against a lawyer who promises to secure for the youth the very fortune which, supposedly inherited by the boy at the beginning of the play, caused him to remain greedily unmoved by the report of his father's death. The boy's uncle, Peniboy Senior, is likewise converted from greed by seeing, as he thinks, "my brother . . . restor'd to life!" (V.6.12). He declares that "None but a *Brother* . . ./ . . . could have altered me:/ . . ./ I thanke you *Brother,* for the light you have given mee" (V.6.32–33, 41). Fraternal as well as filial affection instantly eradicates covetousness, as does a generalized affection toward mankind. The grain-hoarder Sordido, saved from suicide by a group of passing farmers whose curses, when they see whom they have saved, penetrate at last to the after all human core of the miser, repents of his greed, recognizing that "it is that/ Makes me thus monstrous in true humane eyes" (EO, III.8.40–41).

Covetousness is in fact a form of spiritual suicide; only an influx of true emotion can provide nourishment for the soul starving itself to death on a diet of indigestible metal. Sordido realizes just in time what Jonson felt to be man's only means to salvation: "No life is blest, that is not grac't with love" (III.8.57). It is a dictum the force of which can be seen in Jonson's insistence upon mercy in the judging of offenders, and represents the Christian coloring of his Platonic scheme, heightening human love into man's closest approximation of the force which first created a pattern to benefit man.

This exaltation of love as the basis of salvation from impiety is a rather remarkable conclusion to be drawn by a poet the main objection against whom has been that he says nothing about the emotions. The fact of the matter is that Jonson says a good deal about the emotions, but he speaks from the point of view of the philosopher rather than the psychologist. Sordido's reformation is psychologically unconvincing in the extreme, but it is to Jonson philosophically watertight, for an access of brotherly love must put a man in touch with spiritual truth, making it impossible for him to continue a spiritual falsehood. Since covetousness arises only as a substitute for a spiritual drive, the advent of a spiritual drive is bound to displace it. Jonson's interest in this reformation is interest in a symbol rather than in a fact: he wishes to elicit from his audience not a rush of sympathy but a judgment.

The judgment is metaphysical, but the situation presented is practical. Coleridge remarks that Jonson "was a very accurately observing man; but he cared only to observe what was external or open to, and likely to impress, the senses."[8] As so often, Coleridge is perceptive and his perceptions are half right. What Jonson's work, on the surface level, presents is a set of interlocking situations faithful to practical truth. Jonson observed the symptoms and effects of covetousness and portrayed them true to nature. But their importance is not naturalistic accuracy; it is symbolic validity. The covetous men whom Jonson places on his stage are believably covetous; but what is the point of showing a covetous man? For Jonson the point is to utilize and reorder the values of the audience. Everyone knows that covetousness is wicked; now this wickedness is attached to a specific type of person. It is never found as the sole fault in an otherwise good character, never the one callous spot in the otherwise tender emotions of a sympathetic human being. Jonson presents covetousness always in conjunction with an entire syndrome involving emotional sterility and impiety toward the order of Nature. By confining his portrayal of covetousness to a carefully selected group of characters, he equates this prejudged wickedness with a set of other qualities not yet evaluated, forcing an adverse value-judgment which extends into the realm of the metaphysical.

8. Samuel Taylor Coleridge, *Coleridge's Miscellaneous Criticism,* ed. Thomas Middleton Raysor (Cambridge, Mass., 1936), p. 46.

Jonson's characters can be judged in this nonlogical manner whether they are at work or at play. The miniature obsession of a game unwinds their limited concerns as completely as a major obsession coils them together. In the games his characters play we witness one more example of Jonson's practical truth: an event which could have happened and which, under the circumstances, is likely to have happened, which violates no practical criteria in being said to have happened, which, by its verisimilitude, convinces us that in fact it has happened—but which is informed by a metaphysical truth constituting, elegantly, its *façon de parler* and its *raison d'être.* In literature not primarily concerned with judgment upon its protagonists, the revelatory pastime is out of place. In the unselected events of day-to-day life, it seldom occurs in a simple form. We might come across a gardener enjoying a round of Snakes and Ladders, but he would be a rare find. The group bent over a Monopoly board is not composed of real estate tycoons, and the loser at Old Maid is an unmarried aunt only if the children are tactless.

Jonson is in this respect magnificently tactless. The results of his characters' games state with embarrassing clarity the limitation of the players and the limited system of values in their society. When the courtiers of Gargaphie pass over *riddles, purposes,* and *prophecies* to play *"Substantives,* and *Adjectives" (CR,* IV.3.81–88), we are immediately intrigued, for the game cannot help being about the players: Hedon and Asotus, Phantaste and Philautia, are no more than substantivized adjectives themselves. Sure enough, when called upon for an adjective to modify the noun later to be disclosed, each courtier produces a word revealing either his greatest hope—Philautia, "Popular"; Asotus, "well-spoken"; Amorphus, *"Pythagoricall"* (an affectedly learned choice alluding to "signior *Pithagoras,* he thats al manner of shapes" [*EI,* Quarto, III.4.174–75])—or his best-concealed fear: Argurion the ennobler, "Humble"; Hedon the exquisite, "Barbarous"; Anaides the impudent, "White-liver'd" *(CR,* IV.3.94–104). When this amiable little society is not thus split into self-centered units, it spreads before us the range of its collective imagination: weary of Substantives and Adjectives, the courtiers turn to *"A thing done,* and *Who did it,"* anatomizing the concerns of the group. The thing done, like the noun in the game preceding, is withheld until the end;

meanwhile, Asotus believes he "would have done it better," and Argurion declares it was done "Last progresse," both retaining a certain amount of self-involvement. But even more important than self-involvement in this game is the way in which the modifiers arrange themselves like iron filings around the magnet to which all thoughts are drawn: the unnamed act was done "By a travailer," "with a glyster" ("a suppository . . . The pipe or syringe used in injection" [Shorter OED, s.v. Clyster]), "For the delight of ladies," and occasioned "A few heate drops, and a moneths mirth." When the action performed turns out to be the delivery of an oration, Asotus remarks for all, "This was not so good, now," and the game is dropped as the company relapses into ennui (IV.3.160–207).

The sexual preoccupation of *"A thing done"* receives confirmation from the hobbies of which Hedon boasts:

> He courts ladies with how many great horse he hath rid that morning, or how oft he hath done the whole, or the halfe *pommado* ["the *pomado* was vaulting on a horse, the *pomado reversa* vaulting off again"][9] in a seven-night before: and sometime . . . how many shirts he has sweat at *tennis* that weeke. *(CR,* II.1.63–68)

The effect all this sweating and leaping is supposed to have on the ladies is relatively plain. Hedon's avocations supplement the parlor games in measuring the limited radius of interests within which each courtier confines himself, as well as the extent to which the society as a whole is circumscribed by its view of life. None of the courtiers has an inkling of any potentiality in intimacy between men and women other than a few heat drops and a month's mirth. At the same time there is a suggestion of impotence in these creatures who confine and reduce the expression of love, without which "No life is blest," to a game played and who played it.

The singular knight Puntarvolo in *Every Man out* also reduces love to a game, a let's-pretend of courtly stylization. He is married but delights to "court his own lady, as shee were a stranger never encounter'd before . . . and make fresh love to her every morning" (II.1.138–41). The conception sounds appealing until its execution is witnessed. Puntarvolo, returned

9. Commentary on *CR,* II.1.64–65, in HS, *9,* 499.

from hunting, has his wife called to the window and presents his addresses to her from below:

> I have scarse collected my spirits, but lately scatter'd in the admiration of your forme; to which (if the bounties of your minde be any way responsible) I doubt not, but my desires shall find a smooth, and secure passage. I am a poore knight errant (lady) that hunting in the adjacent forrest, was by adventure in the pursuit of a hart, brought to this place; which hart (deare Madame) escaped by enchantment.
>
> (II.3.43–50)

On and on he goes with his "chapter of courtship, after sir LANCELOT, and queene GUEVENER [sic]" (II.3.67–68). This artificial glamour which Puntarvolo superimposes upon an essentially unglamourous relationship wards off the contempt of familiarity with the tedium of superficiality. There is no communication, no reality at all, in his prepenned speeches. Such a game-relationship denies, instead of fostering, the mutual concern of human beings.

That seems, in fact, the purpose of all the games Jonson's characters play. The game of Vapours, the rule of which is "Every man to oppose the last man that spoke: whethe⟨r⟩ it concern'd him, or no" (BF, IV.4, marginal note to 32–38), seems a less highly developed form of Jeering, in which "We jeere all kind of persons/ We meete withall, of any rancke or quality,/ And if we cannot jeere them, we jeere our selves" (SN, IV.1.7–9) —the object being to "speake at volley, all the ill/ We can one of another" (IV.1.24–25). Vapours is a stylization less of derision than of disharmony: men are to be at odds with one another, each taking advantage of the others. It is not a bad emblem of the Fair itself; as usual, the game reveals the concerns and limitations of the society within which it is played. Jeering goes further: it makes a sport not merely of disagreement but of insult. Both practice upon the single-minded concerns of the participants, not for the legitimate purpose of reformation, but with the irresponsible goal of cruel laughter. Neither allows a man any natural weakness: "hee may neither laugh, nor hope, in this company" (BF, IV.4.126–27), for "thou ougsht to grant him nothing, in no shensh, if dou doe love dy shelfe" (IV.4.47–48).

The point of these games is that the players follow the rule: they love themselves and therefore grant nothing to no man. The last thing that would occur to them is to love others and be merciful to their faults. In their satirical exposure of themselves and others they pervert the aim of the satirist; in their jokes they pervert the aim of comedy. For the "moving of laughter," far from being "alwaies the end of *Comedy* . . . is rather a fowling for the peoples delight, or their fooling" *(D,* 2629–31), when dependent upon "what . . . in the language, or Actions of men, is a wry, or depraved" *(D,* 2643–44), "As, also, it is divinely said of *Aristotle,* that to seeme ridiculous is a part of dishonesty, and foolish" *(D,* 2640–42). The true comic purpose is to teach, as the true satiric purpose is "by that worthy scorne, to make them [men] know/ How farre beneath the dignitie of man/ Their serious, and most practis'd actions are" *(CR,* V.1.20–22).

While the satirist is a man who has loved the world, seen its potential splendor, and been bitterly disappointed by its present meretriciousness, the vapourers, and especially the jeerers, have never loved or seen the potential of anything. Peniboy Junior's father calls their game "A very wholesome exercise, and comely./ Like Lepers, shewing one another their scabs,/ Or flies feeding on ulcers" *(SN,* IV.1.34–36). These images of incurable disease, on the one hand, and, on the other, of aggravation rather than treatment for sores which might still be healed, emphasize the culpability of jesters who have no sympathy or wish to help; under their tender care, human failings become hopeless. The basic lack of these men is expressed by Peniboy Junior's father after he has finally routed them:

> as confident as sounding brasse,
> Their tinckling *Captaine, Cymbal,* and the rest,
> Dare put on any visor, to deride
> The wretched. (V.6.7–10)

The jeerers, who have not charity, are become as sounding brass or a tinkling cymbal, for charity is the way to spiritual knowledge: "Follow after charity, and desire spiritual *gifts* . . . that ye may prophesy" (I Corinthians 13:1, 14:1). The poet must possess charity in order to speak truly; the man of noble spirit, in order to act on a heavenly model. It is no wonder that the jeerers, who lack this all-important quality, deride concerns not only earthly but divine, and "with *buffon* licence, jeast/ At whatsoe'r is serious, if not sacred" (V.6.10–11). It is impossible they should know any better.

Charity, sympathy toward one's fellowman, is the emotional expression of that intuition which leads toward the good. The human being who is not drawn to goodness in man (even if submerged) is also not drawn to spiritual goodness; the human being who is will recognize nobility, understand great art, and seek to strengthen the good in other men, while working against the bad. But the players of games in Jonson escape from emotion and responsibility together. Their games are a way of maintaining their own concerns without testing them in the larger world, without involving other human beings in them. The building of a fence against reality proves to be the basic crime or folly of most of Jonson's characters. Whether they do it by retiring into a soundproof house or a stylized game, they withdraw from other men and the action of society. Jonson is a realist insofar as he believes in the importance of mundane reality to spiritual comprehension: for him "the only road past the world of flux leads through it,"[10] not in the Rabelaisian sense that the flux itself provides the meaning of life, but in the Miltonic sense that it is impossible to pronounce without having tasted. Adam Overdo must come to the Fair and acquire knowledge of good and evil before he can judge between them correctly or with the human sympathy necessary to genuine justice. Aloofness from other human beings is not the way to Truth; detachment from those concerns of men which spring from folly must not become detachment from the concerns of men. The poet, the philosopher, or the good man cannot order chaos without knowing of what it is composed. He can only oversimplify it into an artificial design of his own brain, which stands between his "inmost affection" and the practical—which points to the metaphysical—truth.

10. Barish, *Prose Comedy*, p. 184.

4. *Clues to Just Judgment: II*

Speech is the mirror of action.

Diogenes Laertius, *Solon.*

Speech is the image of life.

Democritus, *Idylls.*

The line between what is done and what is said is, in a play, faint
and wavering. Language becomes action: a game played is played in
words; a stance assumed is assumed in speech. So Jonson, who valued—
and wished his audience to value—"matter, above words" *(CR,* Prol.,20),
who labored to reveal "the matter, and foundation" *(D,* 693–94), found
himself caught in a paradox that the visual artist escapes, and envied the
latter that faculty which "orecomes the power of speech, and oratory"
(D, 1527–28). The devices of situation which Jonson uses as standards for
moral judgment seem, in part, an attempt to overcome the primacy of
language and to substitute the primacy of "matter," for although words
are, inevitably, the brushstrokes which Jonson fuses into a picture, it is
not here the language that is of symbolic importance, but the portrait as
a whole: Man at Play, Covetous Man, Noble Man Revealed. The apt
language, like good coloring, convinces us that the picture is what its
title proclaims it to be, but the significance lies in the entire composition.
In these Leaves from Ben Jonson's Emblem Book, the poet approaches as

close as possible to the art which "doth so enter, and penetrate the inmost affection . . . as sometimes it orecomes the power of speech" *(D, 1526–28)*. If the poetry cannot hope to efface itself, it compensates by arranging itself as the harmonious composition of "a speaking Picture" *(D, 1511)*.

At other times, however, Jonson uses the poetic paradox itself as the source of his greatest strength. Since "the matter, and foundation" must be embodied in language, he transmutes language into the matter and foundation: the very words become emblematic. Symbolic action fuses with symbolic language to reveal moral truth.

In *Volpone*, for example, the word "wise" enters the scene almost as soon as the Magnifico himself, who is the first to use it, apostrophizing his gold: "Who can get thee/ He shall be noble, valiant, honest, wise." Mosca confirms the connection: "Riches are in fortune/ A greater good, then wisedome is in nature" *(V, I.2.26–29)*. The kind of wisdom substantiated by Volpone's gold is the sort a fox proverbially possesses: slyness, cunning, opportunism. Once this special definition is established by the circumstances of the word's first use, other characters can be tested by applying the word to them. Voltore does "wisely" to preserve Volpone's love "With early visitation, and kind notes" (I.3.3–4); in his profession he is "so wise" that his tongue "would not wag, nor scarce/ Lie still, without a fee" (I.3.63–65). Corbaccio and Corvino, when they have lost all hope of Volpone's inheritance, are ironically called "wise" for dissembling their joy in what the disguised Volpone insists must be their newly acquired wealth (V.6.25). According to the values of Volpone's world, "'tis fit,/ That wealth, and wisdome still, should goe together" (V.9.19–20). In view of the significance of covetousness, calling a man wise in this play amounts to identifying him as vicious. Even the merely foolish are distinguished by a desire to be "wise." Sir Politique Would-bee styles himself "a wise man" (II.1.1), and although the comment on his journal, "Beleeve me it is wise!" (IV.1.147), is not serious, his desire and the application of the word, even in jest, are warnings that his sort of striving leads toward corruption.

By the same test, Celia is cleared of any possible taint. Her plea for mercy to her would-be seducer, "If you have conscience—," is interrupted

by Volpone: "'tis the beggers vertue,/ If thou hast wisdome, heare me,
CELIA" (III.7.211–12). But Celia has none; the key word will not unlock
the treasury of her favor. She behaves as though she had not heard Volpone's exhortation or any of the promises based upon it, and continues as
before: "If you have eares that will be pierc'd; or eyes,/ That can be
open'd .../ Or any part, that yet sounds man, about you" (III.7.240–42)—
but these are precisely what Volpone does not have, what he has given up
for "wisdom." The extent to which his view of wisdom defines his
fellow characters indicates the degree to which their eyes and ears have
shut out the true wisdom, which is conscience, the "touch of holy saints,
or heaven" (III.7.243).

As Volpone, himself prime symbol of his society's moral stupidity,
is the first to speak the key word "wisdom," so Catiline is the first in his
hypocritical society to mention a visor. He instructs his wife to aid his
political plans and gain allies for him by instituting in their home a
sort of upper-crust bawdy house:

> Get thee store, and change of women,
> As I have boyes; and give 'hem time, and place,
> And all connivence: be thy selfe, too, courtly;
> And entertayne, and feast, sit up, and revell;
> . . .
> . . . It can but shew
> Like one of JUNO'S, or of JOVE'S disguises,
> In either thee, or mee: and will as soone,
> When things succeed, be throwne by, or let fall,
> As is a vaile put off, a visor chang'd. (I.171–84)

The blasphemous comparison with the gods is reminiscent of Ovid's
banquet, at which the disguises merely clarify the masquers' baseness. In
the same way, Catiline's "visor" of lust and luxury grins with the very
expression of his soul. He is deluded in thinking he can put it off at will;
like his patience, that other grimace into which the mask can be con-
torted, "It is a visor that hath poison'd me" (III.171). Catiline thinks of
himself as essentially noble; he passionately hates in Cicero not only his

political opponent but his antithesis, representative of the new order.[1] But in Catiline essential nobility has been marred by the deep-cutting lines of greed, lascivious pleasure, and ignoble patience. His "visor" reveals his inner, and prepares his outer, downfall. As Cethegus remarks when the conspirators are frightened by a sudden darkness and flames, which seem to correspond to the fate they have just been discussing for Rome, "We feare what our selves faine" (I.318).

The same corruption that Catiline begins, with dim understanding, to fear in himself infects the other conspirators, making their overthrow certain before they begin to act. The audience, aware of what the visor represents, recognizes Sempronia's venom and perceives her alignment with Catiline, from Fulvia's description not of her political but of her cosmetical proclivities: "They say, it is/ Rather a visor, then a face shee weares" (II.62–63). Fulvia's own corruption is attested to by her lover, who counters her fit of sulks at his stinginess by threatening to "pluck/ The tragick visor off" (II.277–78).

In a larger sense than he imagines, he does remove her tragic visor, and his own with it. The visor's tragedy is its attempt to conceal what in fact it fatally reveals, from which Curius is saved by his deliberate betrayal of the secret to regain Fulvia's favor, as Fulvia saves herself—and, incidentally, Rome—by betraying the conspiracy to Cicero. Although the secret is so terrible that she "thought, it would have burnt me up" (III.292), Fulvia escapes that end, which Catiline rushes to meet: "Would it [the visor] had burnt me up, and I died inward:/ My heart first turn'd to ashes" (III.172–73). Curius' natural face is restored by Cicero (who himself

1. See especially the middle of Act IV, after Catiline's expulsion from the Senate:

> He save the state? A burgesse son of *Arpinum*.
> The gods would rather twentie *Romes* should perish,
> Then have that contumely stucke upon 'hem,
> That he should share with them, in the preserving
> A shed, or signe-post. (480–84)

And:

> There is no title, that this flattering *Senate*,
> Nor honor, the base multitude can give thee,
> Shall make thee worthy CATILINES anger. (497–99)

possesses "an even face" [V.512] to meet any fortune) when he tells the
young man that "There's nought but faire, and good intended to you;/
And I would make those your complexion" (III.321–22); he is to "blush"
(III.337) along with Cicero for his past misdeeds. Since Curius' new role
as Cicero's spy is to connect him with the Roman senators (whom Cicero
sees as having their "faces . . ./ All bent on me" [V.499–500]) rather than
with the visored traitors, Cicero now refers to Curius' countenance,
though it is deceptive, with the positive value-word: "Keepe still your
former face: and mixe againe/ With these lost spirits" (III.414–15).

    When the play reaches its climax, all visors are torn off: the honest
and the vicious are face to face. Lentulus, now leader of the conspiracy, is
brought before the Senate, confronted by the Allobroges—whose "faces
argue/ Thy guilt, and impudence" (V.177–78), shown a treasonous letter
bearing his seal, the image of his grandfather—whose open countenance
ought to have been, in "his picture,/ . . . of power to call thee from a fact,/
So foule—" (V.169–75)—and, overborne by this impressive collocation
of honest faces, is unable to answer Cicero's triumphant demand: "Where
is thy visor . . . now, LENTULUS?" (V.204). Lentulus has lost face and
visor at once. Since, like all the conspirators, he had no countenance other
than his mask, the moment that is stripped from him, he ceases to exist,
except for the resignation of his aedile-ship and a few colorless words
before he is killed. The tragedy concerns not so much the punishment, as
the impossibility, of deception. In Catiline's final moment he wears no
visor except his own face; but the face, like Dorian Gray's, has, in the
instant before death, taken on all the characteristics of the artifact. The
general (whose "face can bring no ill with't, unto *Rome*" [V.618]) who
has opposed him in battle, as the Senate has opposed Lentulus in the
battle of wits, describes Catiline's final appearance, in his own form at
last:

CATILINE came on, not with the face
Of any man, but of a publique ruine:
His count'nance was a civill warre it selfe.
And all his host had standing in their lookes,
The palenesse of the death, that was to come. (V.642–46)

Deceit contains its own destruction, partly because it corrupts and therefore weakens its practitioner, partly because it becomes the truth. The "civill warre" in Catiline's countenance is not only Rome's but his own—a struggle between the nobility of which he is so keenly aware and the corruption his ambitions have forced him to don and finally permitted to enter his blood. The "visor" which indicates corruption has, in him, become indistinguishable from the "face" which indicates essential nobility. *"Man* is read in his face" *(D,* 522); by wearing a visor, he alters that face and the message it conveys, changes his essence, and destroys himself.

Key words tell the audience who will be destroyed and who saved, and their use shows why. The original usage of such a word or set of words, generally by the play's main character, becomes a standard against which all its subsequent occurrences are measured: the first utterance determines its symbolic value. Thus, in *The Alchemist,* Subtle is the first to employ alchemical jargon; his use of it (though not his insistence on his own powers) is serious, and fixes the terminology as symbolic of a belief in and desire for the ability to outwit nature (I.1.68–79). Sir Epicure's subsequent babble of "our *argent-vive,* the Dragon" (II.1.95), and his inquiries after "the *bolts-head"* (II.2.9) and "the flower, the *sanguis agni"* (II.2.28), mark him out as a total subscriber to this set of values, consequently a man corrupted—a judgment borne out by the content of his speeches. Surly, on the other hand, quotes and rejects the cant of the trade in a lengthy speech (II.3.182–98); his refusal to respect even its usage in good faith, along with his constant plays upon it ("MAM. That's your *crowes-head?* SUR. Your cockscomb's, is it not?" [II.3.68]), solidify his position as skeptic not only of Subtle's art but of the whole theory behind his kind of alchemy—that the processes of nature can be speeded up. But Face, who juggles with the jargon for his own purposes[2] as neither the semibeliever Subtle nor the dedicated skeptic Surly can quite manage to do, is bound to come off better in a world where the criteria of success are intellectual rather than moral. In *Volpone* the final measure of success is the degree of genuine wisdom; in *Catiline*

2. See, for example, II.2.9–10, II.2.254–56, III.4.25–39.

it is the condition of the unmasked countenance; in *The Alchemist,* the greatest actual skill with terms of art—which, considering versatility and control, must easily be granted to Face.

The key word or set of words itself, then, presents an emblem for the play, suggesting not only judgment upon the characters but the nature of the standard applied. *Volpone* is The Play of Wisdom: perversely, only those not called wise are so. *Catiline* is The Play of Masks: those who don them reveal themselves. *The Alchemist* is The Play of Art: those most committed to art are least artful. But within these plays various conclusions are drawn about the position of characters with regard to other sets of values and standards of judgment. These tend to be revealed not by the symbolic identification of a character with a certain usage of a certain word but by the comparison inherent in imagery.

The consistently recurring imagery in *Catiline* provides opportunity to check its effect against that of the key words. The play's basic images are introduced and explained in its epistle dedicatory "TO THE GREAT EXAMPLE OF HONOR, AND VERTUE, *THE MOST NOBLE* William, EARLE OF PEMBROKE," which begins: "MY LORD,/ *In so thick, and darke an ignorance, as now almost covers the age, I crave leave to stand neare your light: and, by that, to bee read.*" This opposite of dark ignorance is the light of understanding and appreciation for the poet— an understanding the twin of which constitutes honor and virtue, rendering its possessor "most noble." Of course, there is much that is archetypal and little that is new in this identification, for the Dark Ages and the Enlightenment are always opposing forces. But Jonson makes poetic capital of the equation by consistently identifying his poet-orator with light, his degenerate noble with darkness.

"Is night/ So heavy on thee . . . ?" (I.1–2), Sylla's ghost asks of Rome as the play opens. The answer is clear: like the thick ignorance that almost covers Jonson's age, night lies over Rome; Sylla has returned "T'ingender with the night, and blast the day" (I.13)—or what is left of it. Catiline's deeds, according to Sylla, have hitherto been "too light" (I.43)—only the murder of a brother, seduction of a sister, or so; he is now to outdo "all the severall ills, that visit earth,/ (Brought forth by night . . .)" (I.49–50), for he carries with him a deadly darkness of his own, luridly illumined:

> Let night grow blacker with thy plots; and day,
> At shewing but thy head forth, start away
> From this halfe-spheare: and leave *Romes* blinded walls
> T'embrace lusts, hatreds, slaughters, funeralls,
> And not recover sight, till their own flames
> Doe light them to their ruines. (I.61–66)

The aim of Catiline's plots is the fall of Rome, the extinction of the light of culture and civilization to make way for the darkness of the soul. In what would be pathetic delusion if he were not impressive beyond pathos, the leader of the forces of darkness imagines himself the source of light, his helpers the heralds of morning:

> Who's there? . . . AURELIA? . . . Appeare,
> And breake, like day, my beautie, to this circle:
> Upbraid thy *Phœbus,* that he is so long
> In mounting to that point, which should give thee
> Thy proper splendor— (I.98–102)

Clearly Catiline believes himself the representative of illumination in a world darkened by shadows of the lowly toiling to the crests of Rome's hills. But Nature herself, who is after all the final judge, confutes him. During the meeting at which the destruction of Rome is planned, "The day goes back,/ . . . / Darknesse growes more, and more!" (I.312–14). The only light that appears is "A bloudy arme . . . that holds a pine/ Lighted, above the *Capitoll!*" (I.320–21). The glaring light that makes Catiline's darkness visible is destructive: in one aspect it is the fire of his spirit in which "My heart first turn'd to ashes" (III.173), now become a torch to light the pyre of Rome, for "I will not burne/ Without my funerall pile . . . / . . . / It shall be in . . . / The common fire, rather then mine owne" (IV.506–10). In its other aspect the flaming torch is the fire of heaven that consumes the conspirators, the brand wielded by "the gods;/ . . . / . . . who, with fire, must purge sick *Rome*/ Of noisome citizens" (III.211–14). This fire flashes out in the night before Catiline's exposure. The lightning storm, sent by the gods to "Tell guiltie men, what powers are above them" (IV.25), leaves Cicero and his supporters alone free from terror, while the corrupt and conniving Roman citizens turn their heads "downe-ward all, like beasts,/ Running away from every flash is made" (IV.9–10).

The real sun of the world is Rome: "this glorious citie,/ The light of all the earth" (V.259–60). The conspirators, more than once compared to Titans, are guilty of overreaching arrogance in their wish to be the source of all brightness, "T'have quench'd the sunne, and moone, and made the world/ Despaire of day, or any light, but ours" (IV.760–61). Catiline's identification of himself with the sun, which turns that sole source of light into destructive fire, both originates and symbolizes the necessity of his downfall, as his assumption of a visor has done. In both cases he is fatally mistaken. As he has failed to recognize the truth represented by the mask, so he fails to realize the significance of his self-identification with the sun: since his identity with *destructive* fire is fixed, that becomes equivalent to "his" sun, and darkness illumined by funeral flames becomes the only kind of day available to him. Just before his death in battle, he actually becomes the sun. For a few moments he ascends to hover over Rome, "And as he riss', the day grew black with him" (V.634); the natural sun is displaced: "The sunne stood still, and was, behind the cloud/ The battaile made, seene sweating, to drive up/ His frighted horse, whom still the noyse drove backward" (V.660–62). But the fiery chariot of Catiline careens too near the earth, threatening to have "Consum'd all it could reach, and then it selfe" (V.664); the driver falls, to "A brave bad death./ Had this been honest now, and for his countrey,/ . . . who had ere fallen greater?" (V.688–90). Meanwhile, Apollo reascends his chariot and the arts ride triumphant through the streets of Rome, saved by the man who can say to its citizens, as he has said on behalf of Fulvia and Curius, "Light 'hem" (III.437).

Imagery, key words, symbolic actions, all mesh into a fine network that covers the surface of Jonson's plays, catching the audience's aesthetic intuition in its threads of nonlogic, closing the net and drawing it upward until there is no escape from the moral judgment the poet has designed.

If Catiline is the Visor-Wearer who, self-deceived, covers his natural parts with corruption, he is also a depraved nobleman, cannot recognize true nobility in others, and deludes himself into thinking that he is the source of all light, while he makes himself the source of all darkness. If Volpone is the Wise One who has lost his natural understanding and desire for true wisdom, he is also a corrupt member of the nobility, has replaced his spiritual drive with covetousness, and spends his leisure being entertained by unnatural beings reciting in doggerel (which he applauds) the soul's loss of divinity and finally of humanity (II.2.1–62). The imagery which surrounds him supports the self-judgment of his diversions: the debasement of classical allusions, the application of Christian terminology to money, the figuring forth of every sort of perverted sexuality, the constant mention of perverted forms of eating—all of which imply the substitution of covetousness for spiritual drives, the loss of true moral comprehension. The strands of imagery, symbolic action, and key word are warp and woof of the play's texture; each is the groundwork of the others.

If Subtle is the false artist whose work attempts to circumvent that of the one true Artist, he is also the covetous man who must be self-involved, whose concerns must be antisocietal and stance one of opposition to the world; and his symbolic covetousness, necessitating aims exactly opposed to those of the good artist, carries us full circle to the implications of the key terminology. The imagery draws its own circle, which is perfectly congruent:

DOL. Yes, say lord Generall, how fares our campe?

FAC. As, with the few, that had entrench'd themselves
Safe, by their discipline, against a world, DOL:
And laugh'd, within those trenches, and grew fat
With thinking on the booties, DOL, brought in
Daily, by their small parties. *(A, III.3.33–38)*

Simultaneously, the impiety inherent in false artistry is confirmed by its greatest patron: "'Epicure', which comes from Greek, and 'Mammon', which is exclusively a Christian term, unite to form a name which is at once a humanistic and Christian comment on impious wealth and immorality."[3] The heresy is confirmed also by sorcerer and apprentice in a Black Mass catechism beginning, "Name the vexations, and the martyrizations/ Of mettalls, in the worke," and culminating in a grand credo:

'Tis a *stone,* and not
A stone; a *spirit,* a *soule,* and a *body:*
Which, if you doe *dissolve,* it is *dissolv'd,*
If you *coagulate,* it is *coagulated,*
If you make it to *flye,* it *flyeth.* (II.5.20–44)

This imagery expresses in words what is expressed in emblematic action by the three main characters: that trinity, coagulated in Lovewit's house, at his return dissolves and is dissolved ("for, here/ Determines the indenture tripartite,/ Twixt SUBTLE, DOL, and FACE" [V.4.130–32]); at least two elements of it Face makes to fly, and they fly.

In an exactly similar way, the symbolic central figure of *Epicoene* is reproduced in a myriad of smaller figures of imagery: the *"hermaphroditicall* authoritie" (I.1.80) of the Collegiate ladies, the neatness of courtiers which surpasses that of "the *french hermaphrodite"* (IV.6.31), the description of Captain Otter as *"animal amphibium"* (I.4.26) and of La-Foole as a "mannikin" (I.3.25). The play's framework sends back the same echo in the names of the latter gentleman[4] and of the Collegiate Lady Centaur. And the diversions of the characters repeat the title word and figure, whether in Mavis' proposed *"Italian* riddle for sir DAUPHINE" (V.2.44), who has devised a typically Italian riddle for Morose, or in Lady Haughty's setting-up exercises with the page:

The gentlewomen play with me, and throw me o'the bed; and carry me in to my lady; and shee kisses me with her oil'd face; and puts a perruke o'my head; and askes me an' I will weare her gowne; and I say, no: and then she hits me a blow o'the eare, and calls me innocent, and lets me goe. (I.1.13–18)

Everything combines to illustrate the rejection of nature, even the covetousness of Morose, who is unnatural not only in displacing the affection

3. Edward B. Partridge, *The Broken Compass* (New York, 1958), p. 149.
4. See above, p. 60.

due his nephew but in assuring that his concerns will be antisocietal and in showing a spiritual perversion away from Nature—the latter implication leading us round again to Epicoene and the imagery.

Jonson's devices are so closely intertwined and form a rope with so powerful a pull in one direction that it is often difficult to classify a passage as employing one device distinct from the others. In Face's description of Dol as a noble lady, for instance, the workmanship is so intricate that the threads cannot be told apart:

> O, the most affablest creature, sir! so merry!
> So pleasant! shee'll mount you up, like *quick-silver,*
> *Over* the *helme;* and *circulate,* like *oyle,*
> A very *vegetall. (A,* II.3.253–56)

Listening to him, we must bear in mind that quicksilver was used to treat venereal disease, while "to the alchemists quick-silver or *argent-vive* and sulphur were 'the parents of all other metalls', sulphur 'supplying the place of male', and quick-silver the place of the female" (II.3.153ff.); and that "circulate," though apt enough already, meant, in addition:

> 'encircle' or 'surround'. It also had a meaning drawn from chemistry: 'to subject a substance to continuous distillation in a closed vessel in which vapour was caused to condense at the top of the apparatus and to flow back into the original liquid, the whole thus undergoing repeated vaporization and condensation.' *(OED)*

This information, its supplier judiciously suggests, "has a certain pertinence," while the vividness of *"'over the helme'* . . . depends on its suggestive vagueness."[5] But every item in Face's report depends for effect on its faithful exactitude (even his use of "circulate" ministers directly to Sir Epicure's hopes that he and Dol will 'renew/ Our youth, and strength . . . / And so enjoy a perpetuitie/ Of life, and lust" [IV.1.163–66]). In view of the definition of "helm" as "the handle or tiller . . . by which a rudder is managed . . . *transf.* Any part which is used like a helm" (the "helm-port" being "'that hole in the counter through which the head of

5. Partridge, *The Broken Compass,* p. 138.

the rudder passes' " [*Shorter OED*]), Face's remarks take on a scandalous precision. Dol emerges clearly as a "vegetall," for she is "characterized by . . . producing the phenomena of physical life and growth."[6]

Such virtuoso use of key language by Face establishes him as probable victor in a Love-Wit world. At the same time, it connects the function of Dol with the terminology of antinatural desire, suggesting that sex in this world is one more form of the attempt to outwit Nature, which leads man toward a contact with his fellow human beings that Dol's kind of love denies or exploits for material gain. In this capacity the key language connects with Face's later description of Dame Pliant to Lovewit: "a widdow,/ . . . / Will make you seven yeeres yonger, and a rich one" (V.3.84–86), for this is the very spirit of alchemy decanted; Lovewit's sexual bargain-hunting incriminates him. But Dame Pliant, though her sexual role resembles Dol's, is not so culpable as she. Dame Pliant's assent to society's evaluation of her is passive and uncomprehending, while Dol provides active justification for the language used about her. The consistent critic (perforce, any critic of Jonson) is obliged to put Face's account of Dol's pastimes, with whatever embarrassment, under the heading "Games." In short, the description involves an artful and inextricable tangle of symbolic action (one must also bear in mind that Face is putting across a concept of *noble* behavior), key words, imagery, and—for without it the imagery would be incomprehensible—punning.

The pun is a form of imagery which convinces through a similarity not between objects but between the sounds of their names. It can be used to establish interrelations, and thus evaluations, in cases not amenable to ordinary imagery. Perhaps this is why such a large proportion of Jonson's

6. *Shorter OED*. This meaning supplements the suggestion in HS that "here Jonson was using (or confusing) it [vegetall] with the Latin *vegetus*" (commentary to II.3.256, in HS, *10*, 85), meaning "brisk, sprightly." Since "vegetall" and *vegetus* are derived from *vegetare* and *vegere* respectively, and the former means "to be animated," as well as having in common with the latter the meaning "to arouse, animate" (Lewis and Short, *A Latin Dictionary*), it seems likely that English and Latin significance combine (as often in Jonson) to characterize Dol as a quick and quickening piece of alchemical matter, who, like Psyche returning from her mission, "vegetior ab inferis occurrit."

purposeful puns (excluding verbal exercises like Cob's recitation of his fishy lineage and confusion of rasher-bacon with Roger Bacon [*EI*, Folio, I.4.10–32]) are sexual allusions. Unmitigated by the comforting possibility that they are only wit, unconcealed by the fig leaf of double entendre, these would appear as naked obscenity; and Jonson considered part of the poet's skill in making men's minds like the thing he writes to depend upon "how hee hath avoyded . . . obscene, sordid . . . *Phrase*" (*D*, 797–99). Indeed, he is explicit on how to avoid it: "by way of . . . *Metaphore*," to be used "when wee avoid losse by it, and escape obscenenesse, and gaine in the grace and property, which helpes significance" (*D*, 1897–1905). All these achievements are facilitated by that specialized form of metaphor, the pun. Exact information on Dol's activities, robbed of alchemical references and reduced to plain English, would have grace and property only in Kinsey; but Face's description escapes obsceneness and helps significance.

Similarly, a later discussion between Face and Subtle on the probable merits of Dame Pliant serves to connect that lady's attractions firmly with the values uppermost in the tricksters' world:

> FAC. A wife, a wife, for one on'us, my deare SUBTLE:
> Wee'll eene draw lots, and he, that failes, shall have
> The more in goods, the other has in taile.

> SUB. Rather the lesse. For shee may be so light
> Shee may want graines. FAC. I, or be such a burden,
> A man would scarse endure her, for the whole. (*A*, II.6.85–90)

The plays on the lady's various possessions make it evident what her best parts are: the equation of primary characteristics sexual and financial confirms the similarity between her function and Dol Common's, suggested by the key terminology, and seals Lovewit's condemnation for later subscribing to the same values.

Dol herself is the source and subject of more puns than those that associate her with alchemy. Face is concerned that she not be recognizable as an experienced strumpet, for her latest admirer "will not pay, not halfe so well" (IV.3.55), unless he can consider himself a seducer; to that end Face exhorts Dol: "You must goe tune your virginall, no loosing/ O'the least time" (III.3.67–68). His instructions make clear not only her main role as well-bred young lady, obedient, in the long hours after dinner, to the metronome ("no loosing/ O'the least time"), but also the importance of her supporting role as a hitherto unplayed instrument. At the same time, his words contain also the very opposite suggestion, as Partridge points out[7] by quoting *Every Man in:* "I can compare him to nothing more happely, then a Barbers virginals; for every one may play upon him" (Quarto, II.3.183–85).

These puns contribute to the texture of language in *The Alchemist*. They are one of the threads which tie actions and characters into packages carefully labeled as to value. But what has been remarked about a different aspect of Jonson's linguistic technique also holds true for puns:

> In the period of his maturity, there was no monotony in his application of the method. But in his last plays, when the quality of the language no longer forms a consistent commentary on the characters and action, the method fails. Dramatic irony is no longer produced in direct proportion to ... the language.[8]

To be sure, when the momentary restoration of Dol's innocence is paralleled by the attempted restoration of Placentia's with the aid of her lover, Needle *(ML)*, the punning imagery of her fiancé's declaration that he will not "take a wife,/ To pick out Mounsieur *Needles* basting threds" *(ML, V.10.115–16)*, fits every aspect of the situation and passes ironic judgment on all participants, even confirming the baseness of Placentia's birth (and character) by incorporating her into an image of tailoring. But Compasse's coarse language to Pleasance in the same play is distasteful and invalid. When Face says of Dame Pliant that "I knew, the Doctor would not leave,/ Till he had found the very nick of her fortune" *(A, IV.4.1–2)*, he contributes one more stroke to our picture of her position in the play's scheme of values; but when Compasse urges his beloved to avoid his rival, "and not acquaint/ A common Lawyer with your case.

---

7. *The Broken Compass*, p. 147, n.1.
8. A. H. Sackton, *Rhetoric as a Dramatic Language in Ben Jonson* (New York, 1948), p. 166.

If hee/ Once find the gap; a thousand will leape after" (*ML*, II.7.9–11),
his language goes completely against her essential nobility, his supposedly
worthy love for her, her innocence, and his name (which should preserve
him from misdirected appraisals). His puns cut across all distinctions the
play seems to be setting up, and render pathetically ludicrous Pleasance's
happy puzzlement: "This riddle shewes/ A little like a Love-trick, o'one
face,/ If I could understand it" (II.7.12–14). This tainting of what is
presented and accepted as a pure love with the same considerations that
have motivated Placentia may indicate either a total obliviousness of the
basic poetic rules Jonson himself has set up, or, more credibly, the flood
tide of a pessimism bubbling in as froth in *The Alchemist* and stemmed
for only a few moments by the magnificent construction of that monu-
mental verbal dike, *Catiline*.

The pun as a source of judgment is found throughout Jonson's mature
plays, but seldom in his earlier works. The play on "Saint Valentine,"
"Sonne Valentine" (an appellation of Awdrey's intended bridegroom,
coined by her father [*TT*, I.3.60]) and "Sin Valentine" ("Hee was a
deadly *Zin* ... / ... / Hee was a stately *Zin*: ... / And kept brave house"
[I.2.8–20]), comes as close to significance as any: it is mildly amusing
and to some degree appropriate, since the play takes place on Saint
Valentine's Day and revolves around the power of infatuation. But even
this pun is not integrally related to the themes of the play or to judgment
on any of its actions. It suggests a much more serious consideration of the
impulses involved than the play ever gives them. In fact, after the initial
pun, the dangers of infatuation get no consideration at all.

In the early plays puns crop up like weeds, which are not pulled out
until we reach the formal gardens of Jonson's maturity. Haphazard word-
play in his first works tends to provide incidental entertainment. It may
achieve an effect of heightening (or lowering), as when Deliro's woeful
tale of his wife's whimsical likes and dislikes takes on unexpected vividness, as a portrayal of marital incompatibility, in his announcement:

Then here, shee hath a place (on my back-side)
Wherein shee loves to walke; and that (shee said)
Had some ill smels about it. (*EO*, II.4.87–89)

But even this occupies at best a subordinate place in the work's thematic structure.

It is not until the mature plays that the pun is set in place as firm moral touchstone. At the entrance to that great period, Ovid's punning last words to Julia can reveal, in the context of the play, his moral decline;[9] at its exit, false religion can be unmasked once and for all even to its practitioner by a puppet's words: *"Nay, I'le prove, against ere a* Rabbin *of 'hem all, that my standing is as lawfull as his; that I speak by inspiration, as well as he"* (BF, V.5.109–11). And in the middle of this period, Subtle's witticism to Dapper, en route to storage in the lavatory: "I now must shew you *Fortunes* privy lodgings" (*A*, III.5.79), can proclaim that in their mutual world, love of money, superseding love of divine favor, has pitched its dwelling in the place of excrement.

Sometimes, especially during this middle period, the pun is used to reflect more indirectly upon the themes of the drama—to make a surprising splash of local color, which is drawn slowly into the fabric of the play. Of this sort is Sir Epicure's pronouncement that when he is rich, his friends need no longer gamble: "You shall no more deale with the hollow die,/ Or the fraile card" (II.1.9–10). His first choice of adjective is derived from the fact that his friends play with loaded dice, but these are the stuffed dice, the hollow dice, which are worthless in both practical function and moral implication. The pun ought to warn Sir Epicure of the vanity of worldly wishes. However, although he seems to recognize the double meaning (in balancing "hollow die" with "frail card"), he does not recognize the overall significance and joyously prepares to go on substituting outer for inner value.

The misguided knight is peculiarly subject to this sort of irony, to which he falls victim again when he announces:

> I doe meane
> To have a list of wives, and concubines,
> Equall with SALOMON; who had the *stone*
> Alike, with me. (II.2.34–37)

9. See above, p. 28.

While he is, of course, referring to Solomon's proverbial wisdom, which gave rise to the opinion, in alchemical circles, that he "had the stone,"[10] "the stone" is also a disease, involving the formation of a stone in the urinary tract. The resulting irritation and obstruction presumably gave the disease its usefulness for bawdy reference.[11] By invoking this meaning, along with the more usual significance of extreme lasciviousness, Jonson suggests at one and the same time that as Solomon's pretensions to lasting glory rest on wisdom, so do Sir Epicure's on lust, and that, furthermore, even Sir Epicure's "itch of mind" (IV.5.93) is really only an impotent itch of body—the search for wisdom degenerated in him into an unproductive mechanical irritation, as in the Alchemist into a futile chemical operation. Throughout the play Sir Epicure's self-deception is underscored by this tendency to make puns whose implication (sometimes along with the pun itself) escapes him. He constantly convicts himself in word as in deed.[12]

The pains which Jonson will take to imbed this kind of ironic revelatory pun deeply into the material of his play and provide it with a suitable setting are strikingly illustrated in *Catiline,* where the device is refined to a new degree of subtlety. Cicero's threat that the old edicts against "a wicked citizen" (IV.199) will be reinvoked: "We have that law still, CATILINE, for thee;/ An act as grave, as sharpe" (IV.200–01), contains a suppressed pun, "act-axe," which is verified two lines later: "the edge of that decree/ We have let dull, and rust." The image of the consul's axe, "a symbol of life and death,"[13] reflects backward on Catiline's earlier description of conditions in Rome:

10. Commentary to *A,* II.1.4, in HS, *10,* 68.

11. The allusion flourished in the seventeenth century. As late as the Restoration, it seems to have been a favorite of Rochester's, who used it to symbolize mental and spiritual impotence (see his *Tunbridge-Wells,* lines 49–56).

12. Compare as the epitome Mammon's self-encouragement before accosting Dol: "Now, EPICURE,/ Heighten thy selfe, talke to her, all in gold" (IV.1.24–25), in which his preparation to attain at once the alchemical, erotic, and oratorical sublime condemns his version of all three kinds of striving.

13. Commentary on *C,* I.360, in HS, *10,* 128.

> the rest,
> How ever great we are, honest, and valiant,
> Are hearded with the vulgar; and so kept,
> As we were onely bred, to consume corne;
>
> . . .
>
> Trembling beneath their rods: to whom (if all
> Were well in *Rome*) we should come forth bright axes.[14] (I.353–60)

Catiline conceives of himself as the axe which is later, in the form of an
Act, turned against him by the state, just as he conceives of himself as
that destructive heavenly fire which later burns him up. The real axe, like
the sun, is a symbol of Rome; and Catiline, far from being her great,
honest, and valiant representative, is one of those "Whom it were fit the
axe should hew in pieces" (IV.281). The same mistaken self-image revealed by Catiline's use of key words and recurrent imagery emerges
when the sound of Cicero's pun makes Catiline's words ring false.

Catiline's own incidental pun, "as we were onely bred, to consume
corne," reinforces his rhetoric only insofar as it displays a quickness of
mind which, to him, justifies his resentment of Cicero's undervaluation.
At the same time, however, the play of wit and the illogical plausibility
lent by a pun to the identity it asserts, and all the pleasure we feel at
discovering a new, adroitly revealed relationship, are concentrated upon
this concept, which Catiline would like to negate. He is not so self-aware
a rhetorician as Cicero, who uses the pun to drive home a concept which
he wants his auditors to credit:

> These purpose to . . .
>   . . . lay wast
> The farre-triumphed world: for, unto whom
> *Rome* is too little, what can be inough? (III.278–81)

If Rome, which sounds like room, does not satisfy the conspirators, that
is surely a clear demonstration of their boundlesss ambition.

---

14. The image is not in Sallust, Jonson's source for this speech, which
has simply "prove terrible" (ibid.).

The importance of these puns is that they convince, not the listeners within the play (who have in general already decided what their positions are), but the audience, which perceives a truth about the speaker and is turned toward or away from his opinion. Similarly, the joint pun of Fulvia and Curius, after the latter's patriotic conversion, justifies his change of heart and affirms the power of Cicero to save by his speech. When Cicero has finished, Fulvia interposes her comment: "He tells you right, sweet friend: 'Tis saving counsaile" (III.406). Scarcely has the audience time to wonder whether she intends the pun, when Curius catches her up: "Most noble *Consul*, I am yours" (III.407), he exclaims, confirming the identity of Cicero with the words of salvation.

The identity of Ovid with the words of "loss of self" ("PUBLIUS, thou'lt lose thyselfe" [P, I.3.46]), on the other hand, is confirmed at the heavenly banquet by the opening of his proclamation: "The great God, JUPITER,/ . . . / Willing to make this feast, no fast/ From any manner of pleasure . . ." (P, IV.5.12–15). "The great God Jupiter," for the purposes of this banquet, is, of course, Ovid; so it is his decree that the feast be no fast. Line division sets this word-play off from the phrase that follows, and we are left, momentarily, with the unqualified statement that this feast is no fast—and with all the religious connotations of "fast" as a sign of piety, humility, desire to please the gods. These associations imply, illogically, that "this feast," which sounds so much like a fast, should be a religious occasion. Since that is exactly what the banquet travesties, the impiety of the game is pointed up by the pun which inaugurates it and lays responsibility for blasphemy at the door of its proclaimer. As is almost always true, Jonson is not content to use one clue to judgment at a time: if he is not combining punning with imagery (as in the allusions to the Consul's axe), he is apt to be blending it into a symbolic action.

The self-deceived, who must be gulled or punished by the end of the play, can be recognized in those who make such puns without realizing their full implications—Sir Epicure, Catiline (not Fulvia or Curius, who intend Cicero's praise), Ovid—and in those to whom such puns are suitably applied. Sir Epicure heads this supplement, too. His conference with Dol, during which she has suddenly assumed the madness that supposedly overtakes her when *"divinitie"* is mentioned in conversation, is interrupted by Face, who checks the knight's effort to calm his lady and keep the Alchemist from hearing her, with his grave comment: "Nay, you must never hope to lay her now" (IV.5.24). He is right from several points of view, the most significant of which is that, in allowing his lust to be aroused (and therefore engaging Dol in conversation), Sir Epicure has raised a spirit beyond his control. His lust is the only specific form of his general greed that has yet had scope for action, and it immediately produces a downfall of sexual expectation, which leads to the downfall of financial expectation, which leads to the downfall of all expectation at the end of the play.

The knight is followed, in the file of those marked out for future discomfiture, by Dol herself, whom Face instructs to "Firke, like a flounder; kisse, like a scallop, close;/ And tickle him with thy mother-tongue" (III.3.69–70). Partridge points out that "the obvious erotic allusion . . . may be reinforced by the pronunciation of 'firke'." Since, as he further remarks, "mother" meant "womb," "mother-tongue" in context acquires the meaning "language of sex"[15]—which is of course the native language of Dol. Never has there been a better application of Jonson's own dictum: *"Language . . .* springs out of the most retired, and inmost parts of us." It "is the Image of the Parent of it, the mind" *(D,* 2031–33). The "mother" of Dol's language, however, is not her mind but her womb; the latter has replaced the former—for this reason "conversation" with her, however intellectual, always finishes by being a sexual matter. This second line of Face's instructions concludes the implied judgment, which the first begins by reducing her to a cold-blooded sea creature. Its pun and imagery deny her not only human emotion but even animal lust. She could hardly be less salacious than a scallop, which "kisses close" only because the mechanics of its shell demand it.[16] As in the pun on "the stone," sexual activity is reduced from the expression of an emotion to a mechanical symptom.

15. *The Broken Compass,* p. 147 and n.2.
16. A fascinating picture of marine life emerges from Jonson's plays. E.g. "shee kisses as close as a cockle" *(CR,* V.4.534); "you [Ananias the Puritan] are an *Otter* [so is the Captain in *Epicoene*], and a *Shad"* *(A,*

The imagery and outright punning in Face's directions to Dol are supported by those attenuated forms of pun, alliteration and assonance. While one should not make devices concerned with so small a portion of a word carry too much weight of specific meaning, it is illuminating to consider, for example, the flabbiness of "writhe, like a flounder; hug, like a scallop, close." The incisiveness of Face's description depends upon the way the words fit together not only in concept but in sound. The "k" and "s" sounds repeating and inverting themselves in "kiss," "scallop," and "close" are not the essential elements which unite those ideas, but as essential sound-elements, they bind the phrase into aural harmony.

The production of this kind of harmony Jonson grants to those of his characters whom we may expect to see victorious. Like apt punning, apt alliteration shows us a man in control of his language, and conscious control—the ability to shape what one says, to say exactly what one wishes, and to say it convincingly—is a complex of abilities on which Jonson put a high premium as signs of self-awareness.

Like Jonson's punning, his use of alliteration and assonance attains maximum meaning in the mature plays, where it contributes to central considerations. In the early works it tends merely to point out for us the areas within which a character's judgment may be trusted—and, of course, those characters whom we can trust at all. When Paulo exclaims:

Now if my love, faire *Rachel*, were so happy,
But to look forth. See fortune doth me grace,
Before I can demaund *(CA,* I.10.1–3)

the concatenation of *f*airness, looking *f*orth, and the grace of *f*ortune— possibly even the fact that his wish is granted be*f*ore he asks—suggests his

---

IV.7.45); Sir Pol is a parrot disguised as a turtle *(V,* V.4); the ancestry of Cob is traceable to "*Herring* the King of fish . . . one o' the Monarchs of the world" *(EI,* Folio, I.4.13–14); the whale in the river above Woolwich lies waiting "(Few know how manie mon'ths) for the subversion/ Of the *Stode*-Fleet" *(V,* II.1.46–49); dolphins give milk "Whose creame do's looke like opalls" *(A,* IV.1.161); and, in buying tobacco, "Who can tell, if, before the gathering, and making up thereof, the *Alligarta* hath not piss'd thereon?" *(BF,* II.6.26–27).

lover's intuition of Rachel's true worth, a point under some dispute in the play. But Paulo seems unconscious of his verbal effects, and these, in turn, are rather trivial. The harmony, such as it is, is spontaneous and fortuitous (for Paulo—not, of course, for Jonson); it contributes more to whatever mild pleasure we feel at Paulo's gentle speech than to a demonstration of any shaping force of mind or will. Moreover, Paulo's next utterance: "how now my love?/ Where is your father?" disrupts the concatenation abruptly. Yet this piece of unawareness is not meant to be funny or to offer any kind of judgment on Paulo.

Every Man in seems already to put more emphasis on alliteration as a product of intellectual control. Knowell Senior is aware of the worth of his son's "free" behavior; Knowell Junior is aware of the worthlessness of his cousin Stephen's pretensions. Both Knowells are aware of their awareness and present it proudly in language that calls attention to itself. Knowell Senior, in keeping with his character as a judicious man, builds his alliteration to a balanced, epigrammatic conclusion:

> There is a *w*ay of *w*inning, more by love,
> And urging of the modestie, then *f*eare:
> *F*orce workes on servile natures, not the *f*ree. *(EI,* Folio, I.2.129–31)[17]

Knowell Junior, whose delight it is to allow his imagination free scope, criticizes his cousin's choice of words in a kind of alliterative aria:

> Your turne, couss? . . . A gentleman of your sort, parts, carriage, and estimation, to *t*alke o' your *t*urne i' this *c*ompanie, . . . like a *t*ankard-bearer, at a *c*onduit! Fie. A wight, that (hetherto) his every *s*tep hath left the *s*tampe of a great foot behind him, as every word the *s*avor of a *s*trong *s*pirit! and he! this man! so grac'd, *g*uilded, or (to use a more fit *metaphore)* so tin-foil'd by nature . . . Come, wrong not the qualitie of your *d*esert, with looking *d*owneward, couz; but *h*old up your *h*ead, so: . . . that men may reade i' your physnomie, *(Here . . . is to be seene the true, rare, and accomplish'd monster, or miracle of nature,* which is all one.) *(EI,* Folio, I.3.107–27)

17. In this and succeeding passages the initial italics (and suppression of italics) are, of course, mine.

Young Knowell's sarcasm is more sophisticated than his father's generalization, though not necessarily more appealing. For young Knowell uses his alliteration to convince, and indeed to deceive, while he does not himself believe most of the implied relations. His sharpness is played off against the dullness of Stephen, who is persuaded not only that "turne" in company makes him a tankard-bearer at a conduit, but that his step is a stamp, his savor that of a strong spirit. Of course the pun passes him by. Of course he misses the verbal joke in which young Knowell—by building up his hearers' auditory expectations with "grac'd" and "guilded," holding them in suspense through a parenthesis, and unexpectedly frustrating them—throws all the emphasis of the sentence on "tin-foil'd." Of course, too, he misses the double meaning of "which is all one" as a clarification of the alliterative identity between "monster" and "miracle." His unconsciousness of the net of wit laid out to trap him, like Sir Epicure's unconsciousness of his own and Face's puns, confirms the justice of his entrapment, for it mirrors the dullness of his ethical faculties. So Knowell Junior, as entrapper, is justified.

But the information that Stephen is a fool is superfluous; that his mind has no controlling force is already obvious. If we get in Knowell Junior's speech some particularization of the area in which Stephen is a fool (his grace and gilding are tinfoil, and he would wish to think of himself as a stamper rather than a stepper), we get also other less functional amusement: the savor of a strong spirit is included for the pleasure of fooling, not of condemning, the uncarousing Stephen.

Indeed, this auditory separation between the just and the unjust provides, in the early plays, mainly immediate amusement; in the later plays, part of the total meaning. To realize that Sir Epicure's richly inventive mind is nevertheless without control or shaping power is to realize something important about his aspirations; and to hear him announce that "with drinking the *elixir*" he will "enjoy a perpetuitie/ Of life, and lust" *(A,* IV.1.164–66) is to hear him make an alliterative equation which is one of the play's themes.

The most complicated such representation of entrapper and entrapped occurs in *Catiline,* where the difference between successful and unsuccessful rhetoric is in some sense the subject matter itself. Here the

standard of error is much higher than in the foregoing plays. Everyone
knows the basic rules of alliteration and assonance and is capable of
operating within them. If Cicero can thank the Senate for "The good, or
greatnesse of your benefit" (III.10), Catiline can urge the conspirators
to "this great, and goodliest action" (I.338). If Cicero judges Rome's
sickness to be "dangerous, and deadly" (III.439), Catiline considers
Rome's most important generals "firme,/ And fast unto our plot"
(I.444–45). Cicero accuses Catiline of "thy mischiefe, and thy madnesse"
(IV.267), and Catiline counts on the "starke securitie" of the common-
wealth and "the whole *Senate*/ Sleepy" (I.436–38). Caesar favors the
conspirators' "actions of depth, and danger" (III.493), the ambassadors of
the Allobroges think that the Senate's tyranny over them is caused by
"our base petitionarie breath/ That blowes 'hem to this greatnesse"
(IV.17–18), and even the Chorus, by no means exceptionally perspicacious, considers Rome's men "More sleek'd, more soft, and slacker
limm'd" (I.562) than her women. In other words, everyone can emphasize
at will simple and logical conjunctions. The criterion of worth is no
longer the mere ability to use such a device but the ability to use it at a
higher level of significance.

The Chorus, as befits the representative of the ordinary well-inten-
tioned man, is a link between those whom language, at this higher level,
leads to their goals and those whom it leads astray. They are capable of
expressing, by a transformation in sound, a transformation in state of
being: *"Romes* faults (now growne her fate) doe threat her" (III.847), and
of seeing that superficial (represented by linguistic) similarities may obscure vital differences in value: "Be more with faith, then face endu'd"
(II.377). But while they comprehend the danger, they do not always
comprehend the crucial distinction: they can be taken in. When their
moral perception has failed them and allowed the conspiracy to gain
ground, they ascribe their confusion to linguistic naïveté: "like men in
mists" (IV.844), they have listened to the voices which slander honest
magistrates,

> And call their diligence, deceipt;
> Their vertue, vice;
> Their watchfulnesse, but lying in wait. (IV.883–85)

When their minds act independently, they are able to distinguish plausible sound from real content, but when they are acted upon by others, they believe the equivalences they hear.

Cicero, on the other hand, is never acted upon but always acting upon others. He is absolutely undeceivable, which is no doubt one reason why he is so smug. His perception of appropriate aural linkages enables him to predict accurately what no one else quite believes of Catiline: "he, before/ Hath safely done so much, hee'll still dare more" (III.245–46). As acute in analyzing the past as the future, he sets his conclusions before Catiline in the Senate with an emphasis he cleverly increases by delaying the clinching word: "Onely, a little let there was, that stay'd thee,/ That I yet liv'd" (IV.290–91). He perceives irony as easily as fact, and conveys it (heavy-handedly but accurately) to Lentulus when the seal of the latter's noble grandfather is found on a treasonous letter: "Was not his picture,/ . . . of power to call thee from a fact,/ So foule—" (V.173–75). Just as he can convincingly set forth the baseness to be feared in the conspirators, so he can convincingly describe the nobility to be sought in himself:

> this *p*oore *l*ife,
>
> . . .
>
> They cannot with more eagernesse *p*ursue,
> Then I with gladnesse would *l*ay downe, and *l*oose,
> To buy *Romes p*eace, if that would *p*urchase it. (IV.83–87)

Plainly what he wishes to purchase is peace, and therefore he considers his life poor; just as plainly, his desire to purchase peace draws enemies to pursue his poor life. And he can easily utilize, like Knowell Junior, the anticlimax created by a sudden lack of alliteration, and make a pointed climax of it: "My fortune may forsake me, not my vertue" (IV.821). Fortune is indeed linked to forsaking; virtue is not.

This facility in rendering evident connections (and discontinuities) which might otherwise be unnoticed or even disputed displays Cicero's intellectual control, and gains him his practical control, over situations and men. He efficaciously convinces the Allobroges that their position as "men, whose *f*ortunes are yet *f*lourishing,/ And are Romes *f*riends," contains an intimate connection between those apparent accidents and

points out to them in a practical way that if they "become her *e*nemies"
the ensuing misfortune will involve "their *e*states" (IV.630–33). As a
result, they agree to spy on Catiline instead of turning to him. Similarly,
Cicero devises a scheme for converting the Consul Antonius from in-
born treachery to patriotism:

> I must with offices, and *p*atience, win him;
> Make him, by art, that which he is not *b*orne,
> A friend unto the *p*ublique; and *b*estow
> The p*rovince* on him; which is by the *Senate*
> Decreed to me: that *b*enefit will *b*ind him.
> 'Tis well, if some men will doe well, for *p*rice. (III.474–79)

Many advantageous connections emerge from this plan: Antonius will
do well because the province is the price his fellow consul's patience has
devised to make the public palatable; and the next best thing to being
born for well-doing is having someone bestow a benefit which will bind
one to good behavior. No wonder Catiline, who had hoped to make
Antonius a creature of his, is forced to answer the query, "How find you
ANTONIUS?" with "The'other ha's wonne him, lost: that CICERO/
Was borne to be my opposition" (III.657–59).

In order to understand the full significance of Jonson's attention to
alliteration in this play, we must place that device in the context of the
mirror-like "opposition" he has set up between hero and villain. Catiline
and Cicero both stand for "ambition," as is more than once pointed out
within the play; but within that concept they stand for opposing principles. Catiline represents false ambition (self-seeking) and Cicero true
ambition (self-transcendence), of which the first is destructive, the
second productive. For "if divers men seek *Fame,* or *Honour,* by divers
wayes; so both bee honest, neither is to be blam'd; But they that seeke
Immortality, are not onely worthy of leave, but of praise" *(D,* 175–78).
If, however, one of them be not honest, his search for honor becomes

> the last affection
> A high minde can put off: being both a rebell
> Unto the soule, and reason, and enforceth

All lawes, all conscience, treades upon religion,
And offers violence to natures selfe. (III.248–52)[18]

Catiline fights for nobility as a standard of virtue, Cicero for virtue as a
standard of nobility; Catiline fights for the old order, Cicero for the
new. They compete for the consulship, for the loyalty of Antonius, for
the sympathy of the Allobroges, and for the life of Rome. Each has one
prime supporter more zealous than he is himself against the opposition
(Cato and Cethegus), each employs one of the two self-enamored
courtesans in the play, and each has in his party one important man who
is actually in sympathy with the other (Caesar and Curius). But in each
of these parallels the advantage falls on Cicero's side. Cethegus' zeal fails
to kill Catiline's opponents; Cato's gets the conspirators sentenced to
death. Sempronia, aging and unattractive, talks without effect; Fulvia,
young and seductive, elicits the first information about the conspiracy
and brings it to Cicero. Cicero knows that Caesar favors Catiline; Catiline
has no idea that Curius favors Cicero.

This uneven parallel extends to their utterances. When Cicero has
demonstrated for the first time (but by no means the last) his sincere
didacticism ("The vicious count their yeeres, vertuous their acts"
[III.83]), the next scene finds Catiline aping Cicero's style and temporarily outdoing the original: "It is a kind of slander, to trust rumour";
and, "They are no lesse part of the common-wealth,/ That doe obey, then
those, that doe command"; and, "Who's angrie at a slander, makes it true"
(III.140, 133–34, 143)—the last closely resembling Cicero's later, "Justice
is never angry" (V.599). While Ciceronian piety and wisdom flow from
Catiline's lips, they are, of course, ineffectual: he is incapable of seeing
the truth of his own statements.

Jonson provides us with more exact echoes to make sure we grasp
the distorted parallelism. Cicero's interview with his informants is
followed by Catiline's with the conspirators (Fulvia and Curius linking

18. The parallel with Milton's "*Fame* is the spur that the clear spirit doth
raise/ (That last infirmity of Noble mind)" *(Lycidas,* lines 70–71) should
be pointed out for the sake of completeness though not of originality.

the scenes by playing both roles). And just as Cicero's ends with a
soliloquy lamenting

> that the first symptomes
> Of such a maladie, should not rise out
> From any worthy member, but a base
> And common strumpet. . . .
> . . . Thinke, thinke, hereafter,
> What thy [Rome's] needes were, when thou must use such meanes.
>
> (III.448–53)

so Catiline's meeting prompts his equivalent soliloquy:

> What ministers men must, for practice, use!
> The rash, th'ambitious, needy, desperate,
> Foolish, and wretched, ev'n the dregs of mankind,
> To whores, and women! (III.714–17)

But whereas Cicero takes this circumstance to be a sign of the corruption of the state and attributes Rome's need of Fulvia to the scorn of
the gods "When they will show thee what thou art" (III.454–64), Catiline,
with less humility and less self-knowledge, concludes,

> still, it must be so.
> Each have their proper place; and, in their roomes,
> They are the best. (III.717–19)

Being unaware of what constitutes corruption, he naturally cannot control
it. So his attempt to establish himself even superficially as the minister
of light must fail: Cicero can dismiss his spies by commanding the
servants to "Light 'hem" (III.437), but Catiline attempting the same
gesture is foiled by the nature of evil:

> CAES. You shall not stir for me. CAT. Excuse me, lights there.
> CAES. By no meanes. CAT. Stay then. (III.526–27)

This crucial difference in the ends for which the conspirators and
Cicero use their rhetoric and, particularly, in their understanding of
those ends is reflected in their control over so small a matter as allitera-

tion. Here, as everywhere, the conspirators' style mirrors but distorts Cicero's. Catiline, too, talks of what may be done with a province; he asserts that his opponents covet

> new-found gemmes,
> Since POMPEY went for *Asia,* which they purchase
> At price of *provinces!* (I.386–88)

But Catiline's pretensions in this speech to the role of righteous judge are undercut when we hear Cicero employ the same alliterative terms to sacrifice a province—not for his pleasure, but for the good of the commonwealth—and substitute for Catiline's simple concatenation the much more subtle connections Cicero intends to set up between the "province" and the "publique" and his own "patience."

It is as though Jonson took pains to disqualify not only the content of the conspirators' speech but its very form. Of course falseness of form follows from falseness of content: since they misjudge the truth of things, they arrange them in fallacious patterns. So Cicero, aware of the true value of Fulvia, can manipulate assonance to flatter her without confusing himself:

> her very name will be a statue!
> Not wrought for time, but rooted in the minds
> Of all posteritie. (III.352–54)

Here Fulvia plays the role filled earlier by Stephen; she cannot resist the conviction carried by sound.[19] Catiline, however, attempting to use the

19. Cicero's verbal pattern here is as false as those of the conspirators, but his conscious control is crucial:

Another slander is to the effect that no art will acquiesce in false opinions: since an art must be based on direct perception, which is always true: now, say they, rhetoric does give its assent to false conclusions and is therefore not an art. I will admit that rhetoric sometimes substitutes falsehood for truth, but I will not allow that it does so because its opinions are false, since there is all the difference between holding a certain opinion oneself and persuading someone else to adopt an opinion. . . . an orator, when he substitutes falsehood for the truth, is aware of the falsehood and of the fact that he is substituting it for the truth. He therefore deceives

same verbal technique to characterize *his* aides, ends up in the position
of Fulvia rather than Cicero:

> Shall CATILINE not doe, now, with these aides,
> So sought, so sorted, something shall be call'd
> Their labour, but his profit? (III.731–33)

Catiline's aides, though he has sought them, are anything but "sorted":
they are a miscellaneous group and have not been discriminated among
(indeed, they include a secret traitor); they are ill-sorted and constantly
disagree with one another as to methods; and they are not suited to the
tasks entrusted to them. Here Catiline shows himself a greater dupe than
the less intelligent Chorus: their perceptions are accurate when not
wrought upon by deceivers, but Catiline deceives himself.

Lentulus displays a further degree of this characteristic self-deception
when, like his leader, he botches a pattern Cicero can easily command.
When Cicero accuses Catiline of having wished before to kill the chiefs
of state, "when not thy *f*eare, nor *c*onscience chang'd thy mind,/ But
the meere *f*ortune of the *c*ommon-wealth" (IV.338–39), he underlines
the lack of decent motive by substituting an alliteratively identical
replacement. But Lentulus does not even realize that he is performing
the same substitution when he supplements a description of some
potential supporters' motivations: "their *h*ope of *l*ibertie," with "Or
*h*ate unto their *l*ords" (III.610–11). The meanness of the conspiracy,
the reducibility of all its slogans to simple resentment for superiors, is
laid bare with one blundering stroke. It seems as though the conspirators
can be forced into alliteration by the truth of things. So Caesar fixes not
the motives but the fate of the conspiracy in an ill-chosen piece of alliterative scorn at Cicero's watchfulness: "Would you have/ Such an
HERCULEAN actor in the scene,/ And not his HYDRA?" (III.99–100).
This witty remark finds a double echo later in the play, when Catiline
repeats its gist in the Senate with equal unawareness: "What doe you
make him, CATO, such a HERCULES?" (IV.478), and Cicero ap-

---

others, but not himself. (Quintilian, *Institutio Oratoria,* II.17.17–20, trans.
H. E. Butler, Loeb Classical Library [London, Wm. Heinemann, 1921])

propriates the comparison at last, revamping the alliteration to reveal its true force: "we must so provide,/ That, while we take one head, from this foule *Hydra,/* There spring not twentie more" (IV.531–33). The conspirators' language, as usual, has slipped from their control, and it must come as an unpleasant surprise to them that in fact *they* are the Hydra on the brink of decapitation.

In short, although the conspirators are capable, like everyone else in the play, of recognizing and expressing simple factual correspondences, they are not capable, as Cicero is, of seeing the implications of more subtle ones or creating new conjunctions which have fruitful consequences. At most, they may succeed in effective self-denigration. So Catiline can speak of "dull, stupide LENTULUS,/ My stale, With whom I stalke" (III.722–23), and Cethegus, ever contemptuous of the conspiracy's methods, can declare, "These wishings tast of woman, not of *Romane*" (III.182). But let them venture into the realm of prediction, or sarcasm at Cicero, or praise of themselves—any of the realms in which they are self-deceived—and their language is undercut not only by immediately evident falseness but, most often, by Cicero's appropriate use of a similar turn of phrase.

This is, of course, a special form of verbal irony. The false statements of the conspirators would be false even if they did not alliterate, and the unwittingly accurate ones would retain their unnoticed truth. But the triumphant emphasis that the conspirators insist on giving these utterances, the claims to judgment and wit implicitly entered by what evidently seems to them verbal virtuosity, makes every speech of this kind a dramatic action in itself, in which we see—or rather hear—in miniature the fatal unawareness of the speaker and his inevitable doom. The more the conspirators attempt, in their verbal linkings, to impose a false pattern on events and circumstances and values, the more sharply they set off the true pattern that relentlessly emerges beneath and around the language in which they think they have confined it. And, of course, the presence of Cicero, easily putting to its right use each device that the conspirators stumble over, picking up their misused words and returning them to their proper contexts, completes the verbal interaction of this most language-conscious of dramas.

Because *Catiline* makes language so completely identical with action (its dramatic climax is the heroic delivery of a seven-page oration), it must fail on the stage. On the other hand, it provides, for the same reason, a perfect measure of the lengths to which Jonson was willing to go to achieve verbal and moral congruence. The "richness . . . that is Ben Jonson's distinction" lies in this marvelous ability to interrelate the verbal and conceptual "facts" on the surface of his plays into an unbelievably intricate mosaic exactly representative of the world as he sees it. The picture, comic or tragic, is colored by irony, which "in Jonson is . . . not limited to isolated scenes or dependent merely upon a conventional disguise. It arises from an ironic view of life in which vice and folly among men seem constantly to expose themselves."[20] This self-exposure, along with the revelation of goodness, is achieved and guaranteed not only by the structural techniques discussed in the second chapter, above, but also by the symbolic and metaphorical devices of situation and language.

Only a fragmentary selection of these has been explored; the mine is hardly emptier than before. Nothing at all has been said about rhyme. We have not investigated the possibility that Jonson employs a "negative catalogue" that

> lists attributes not possessed by the object or situation under discussion . . . carefully formed into a commentary on possibilities which might be, but are not. The contrast by negation presents no desirable values but evils which may be realized and happen, for the moment, to lack prominence.[21]

We have not dealt with devices of form, such as the invocation of a certain type of speech by the form of one delivered, which is to be judged by the relationship: for example, the impious catechism of Face by

20. Sackton, *Rhetoric,* pp. 162, 165.
21. Enck, *Comic Truth,* p. 118. One wishes that Enck had supported this description with even one example to encourage prospective followers.

Subtle, the blasphemous morning hymn of Volpone to his gold, the in-
side-out formal farewell speech of Sir Epicure to a way of life.[22]

These, like the devices we have investigated, are part of Jonson's
"poetry of the surface," in which "unconscious does not respond to unconscious; no swarms of inarticulate feelings are aroused."[23] But swarms
of semiarticulate judgments are aroused, not the least of which is the
judgment that judgment itself must be based on experience (which the
plays constitute) and charity (which the judgments of their characters
illustrate). The significance of Jonson's brilliant surfaces is the exactness

22. Compare Sir Epicure's promotion of his friends:

> This day . . .
> You shall no more deale with the hollow die,
> Or the fraile card. No more be at charge of keeping
> The livery-punke, for the yong heire, that must
> Seale, at all houres, in his shirt. No more
> Shall thirst of satten, or the covetous hunger
> Of velvet entrailes . . .
>   . . . make
> The sonnes of *sword,* and *hazzard* fall before
> The golden calfe, and on their knees, whole nights,
> Commit idolatrie with wine, and trumpets:
> Or goe a feasting, after drum and ensigne.
> No more of this. *(A,* II.1.8–24)

with Othello's demotion of himself:

>   O, now for ever
> Farewell the tranquil mind! farewell content!
> Farewell the plumed troop and the big wars
> That make ambition virtue! O, farewell!
> Farewell the neighing steed and the shrill trump,
> The spirit-stirring drum, the ear-piercing fife,
> The royal banner, and all quality,
> Pride, pomp and circumstance of glorious war!
> And, O you mortal engines, whose rude throats
> The immortal Jove's dread clamours counterfeit,
> Farewell! Othello's occupation's gone! (III.3.345–57)

23. Eliot, *Elizabethan Essays,* pp. 66–67.

with which they fit their substructures. At its best, the poetic surface of one of Jonson's plays is in no sense a veneer, but the most finished presentation of the grain itself. No color, no polish, is expended for its own sake; they are there solely to heighten the observer's perception of natural shape and texture. For "the order of Gods creatures in themselves, is not only admirable, and glorious, but eloquent; Then he who could apprehend the consequence of things in their truth, and utter his apprehensions as truly, were the best Writer" (D, 2129–30). The best writer was what Jonson strove to be. Eliot, looking more closely at his great predecessor, pronounces a juster judgment: "We cannot call a man's work superficial when it is the creation of a world."[24]

For the spectators who survey Jonson's world, unconscious responds to consciousness. The devices with which we have dealt suffice to show how Jonson secures the consent, not strictly speaking of the intellect, but of the aesthetic and so the moral judgment. The logic of these techniques is alogical: its position convinces like that of the hands on the dial which one notes without analyzing the manner of its achievement. Yet this special logic is no more implausible than that of any form of metonymy: partial resemblance is made to seem total likeness. In a human or inanimate object, one trait—whether it be a sound occurring in the name (in alliteration and assonance), the whole name (in punning), one or more characteristics of the object (in imagery), its relation to a specific set of words (in key terminology), or one behavioral tendency (in symbolic action)—is made to convince the hearer of the object's total value either by relating it to another (by alliteration, assonance, punning, imagery) whose value is known or easily deducible, and so transferring to the original object all the qualities of the second, or by making the single trait stand for an entire complex (through key terminology or symbolic action). While the first set of devices, those of comparison, move from the unknown to the known (she who firks [value unknown] is like a flounder [animal, cold, movement not dictated by emotion]), the second set, those of symbolism, move from the known to the unknown (he who plays at "jeering" [cruel, uncharitable, per-

24. Ibid., p. 79.

verse] is a jeerer in his view of the world [value previously unknown]),
and both force a value judgment on what has, before the application
of the poet's techniques, not been amenable to convincing evaluation.

In this way the poet avoids the endless regression which keeps the
philosopher wearily marching. To the question, But *why* is this good
or not good? the poet replies, not with a reasoned definition subject to the
same question, but with a demonstration that "this" is just like (or unlike)
something else of whose pleasant or unpleasant qualities the audience
is already convinced. If, like Jonson, he also adheres to an intuitive
epistemology, he can be reasonably sure that the audience will have such
convictions and that they will be right. He can cut off the endless "why"
by replying that man's instinctive orientation toward an absolute Good
enables him to judge rightly at least in simple matters; that the poet's
task is to strengthen that intuition by leading it from such simple
evaluations to far more complex moral judgments; and that the aesthetic
recognition to which poetic logic appeals is also present in every man,
because it is the twin of that moral recognition the poet activates, both
born of the impulse toward the Good which makes man human.

Conclusion: The Uses of Integrity

Sweet are the uses of integrity,
Which, like the toad, ugly and venomous,
Wears still a precious jewel in his head.

> Adap. fr. William Shakespeare, *As You Like It*, II.i

There is a line among the fragments of the Greek poet Archilochus which says: 'The fox knows many things, but the hedgehog knows one big thing'. . . . taken figuratively, the words can be made to yield a sense in which they mark one of the deepest differences which divide writers and thinkers, and, it may be, human beings in general. For there exists a great chasm between those, on one side, who relate everything to a single central vision, one system less or more coherent or articulate . . . and, on the other side, those who pursue many ends, often unrelated and even contradictory . . . related by no moral or aesthetic principle.[1]

Jonson is one of those rare thinkers who combine the metaphysical hedgehog and the practical fox. He knows many things about the real world; he pursues his characters pursuing their ends, which are unrelated, most often contradictory, and immoral in the extreme. But they are important to him, are judged by him, for their relation to the truth,

1. Sir Isaiah Berlin, *The Hedgehog and the Fox* (New York, Simon and Schuster, 1953), pp. 1–2.

that "one big thing" which he felt that he as poet could see and must communicate, without which all the actions of the world are vanity. In dedicating the structure of his dramas to ordered Nature, and their devices (symbolic and metaphorical) to intuitive perception of ultimate value, he resolves that major problem of the satirist, "to create an ordered disorder . . . present us with a rabble to suggest the multiplicity of vice and its chaotic nature, but . . . also find at the same time some way of preventing his own composition from being ultimately as fragmentary as the world it mirrors."[2]

But even a Seer must have nourishment: Jonson fed upon the acceptance which heralded his vision—scanty fare. This diet of gruel—for even in his greatest successes least attention seemed paid to what he considered most vital—probably played its part in the attenuation of the vision. Potentially it was a vision of glory; for precisely in burdening man with total responsibility, it awarded him limitless potentiality, surrounded him with a universe which fostered his impulses toward the Good, and conspired to make him, if he would consent, partly divine. He could, by intervention of the poet, know the truth, and the truth would set him free of every element unworthy the good man, that lover of beauty, of right reason and action, of his fellowman.

Inability to accept imperfection is a distinguishing characteristic of those who love too well, whether the beloved is a human being or the world of human beings. In such cases the lover has a choice of adhering to the vision or compromising with the reality before him. Jonson adhered to the vision. Necessarily, he sacrificed temporal happiness to spiritual conviction, and earthly to intellectual beauty. If Truth fails of its effect on man, the lack must be in man, not in Truth. In order to maintain the cosmic optimism of his vision, Jonson was forced to judge more and more harshly of the world around him. He had too much common sense not to see that practical improvement wrought by art was minimal, and too much idealism to accept the world as being necessarily the sublunary anthill he felt it to be actually. The artist's duty, his function, was, for Jonson, to combat evil; but he perceived the possibility that the task was hopeless.

2. Kernan, *The Cankered Muse,* p. 86.

The structure of his plays remains the same, yet man's position slips downward. The artist and the judge artistically endowed disappear. Evil, once washed away in the tide of understanding, noble and aesthetic *(CA, EI, EO, CR)*, becomes a stubborn stain, to be kept from discoloring society only by banishment or destruction of the tainted offenders. While *Poetaster* hovers between purgative medicine and surgery for society's ills, the artist is still present, still successful in creating and upholding a noble society. In *Sejanus* he has disappeared. To depict the artist as unsuccessful would have compromised the picture of the true poet, for his effect, ideally, is part of his definition; in an incurable society, therefore, Jonson could not show him. His final appearance, in *Catiline,* is a formidable attempt at reinstatement. The unheroic usurpers who make *Volpone* an animal kingdom, and the golden rule of *The Alchemist* a comic version of *Sejanus'* tragic statement, are scattered by sheer force of intellect. The magnificent construction of *Catiline* seems a final effort—built rather on desire than on conviction—to reach the stars, which had originally seemed so near. Cicero as representative of Truth sometimes strains belief nearly to the breaking point: he sets spies; protects and conciliates Caesar, known to be a traitor; bribes his fellow consul; practices upon Fulvia shameless flattery and flat deception; protests feelings he never felt. All Jonson's rhetorical strength is needed to keep the audience's sympathy, even judgment, on the right side. All his poetic devices are marshaled, with a consistency that defies the slightest break in the ranks, for support of the chosen position. It is a position he never takes again.

The disappearance of ideal man and ideal society from Jonson's dramas has led to the assertion that

> the satiric tendency to insist on the gulf between things as they are and things as they ought to be wanes noticeably in the course of his career, and his attitude becomes more and more that of the man whose recognition of folly in himself prevents him from judging it too harshly in others.[3]

3. Barish, *Prose Comedy,* p. 146.

However, the only play which lends credence to this view is *Bartholomew Fair,* and only if one allows the dust raised by Jonson's fighting a double battle to obscure the movements of the enemy. If Puritans are castigated, it does not mean that Vapourers are accepted. If the uses of the flesh must be acknowledged, its abuses are not therefore denied. Adam Overdo must taste the apple of knowledge, but that does not exonerate the snake. In fact, it is Overdo and Rabbi Busy and Dame Purecraft who are capable of amendment, while Ursula and her brood remain unchangeable. A misdirected impulse toward the Good is still more to be valued than none at all.

Despite the sparkling eyes with which he surveyed the fleshly world and the expert movements with which he traversed its paths and burrows, Jonson never became one of its foxes. He loved its nonspiritual vitality, devoid of moral significance; still he felt its self-degradation and betrayal of his spiritual standards keenly enough to write the *odi et amo* of his later works that has so confused, even antagonized, critics. Gems of invention and brilliantly eccentric flashes of characterization were never displayed in more profusion than in *The Staple of News* and *The Devil Is an Ass,* but here they are set in tarnished metal. The sudden, unconvincing reformation of Peniboy Junior and his uncle does not outbalance the convincing inhumanity of the Jeerers, who, though momentarily routed, continue at large (like Dol and Subtle) in a world the stupidity and pettiness of which has been amply testified to in the News Office. Those who are cured and those who are put to flight constitute the merest fraction of a society entirely composed of their unsavory likes. In *The Devil* the situation is yet more hopeless. The position of the most nearly good characters is a distorted recapitulation of Celia's and Bonario's, forced out of shape by the material available in this narrowed human world. Wittipol, though concerned to rescue Mrs. Fitz-Dottrell from the outrages of her husband, avowedly expects to gain her for himself. To further his desires, he recommends himself as an accomplished lover (I.6.199–202) in exactly the kind of seductive language which condemns Volpone's suit to Celia, gives a certain sum of tender payment on account (II.6.71–78, marginal note), and embellishes further promissory statements with the sort of animal imagery (II.6.74–79) that has passed judgment on the world of *Volpone* and *Sejanus*. True, his friend Manly is hidden behind the arras when the crisis comes, to prevent total defection from morality; true again, his services are not needed, because of Mrs. Fitz-Dottrell's unpredictable disinclination; but set against the couple's previous behavior, the lady's righteous exculpation before her husband becomes victory on a technicality. At the same time, sympathy with Mrs. Fitz-Dottrell in her galling marital situation prompts our dismay when she is (unlike Celia) returned to her husband.

There is no longer any genuine triumph of goodness or any escape from doltishness. Mrs. Fitz-Dottrell's return to the connubial hearth does not mean, however, that her husband's version of marital bliss is accepted by Jonson. It is unacceptable, but it cannot be altered. The man is capable of nothing better. There is no suggestion anywhere in Jonson, whether in his works proper, his prologues and epilogues, his dedications, his correspondence, or his conversations—so far as we possess all these— that he had any propensity to pardon folly in others or the slightest recognition of it in himself. On the contrary, he seems to have grown more bitter against it as he grew older, and more jealous of what he considered his due esteem. More and more he looked to the "reader extraordinary" for understanding, convinced that he could not find it in the mass of Fitz-Dottrells who made up the bulk of the world. His attitude is indicative of what his plays confirm—a growing disbelief in the possibility of virtue, bringing with it poetic discrimination.

I do not mean to suggest simply that Jonson's disposition, originally sunny, was clouded over by the mist of unpopularity, his essential sweetness soured. The conflict between the glory of what ought to be and the mundane reality of what could be was inherent in his satiric position, but he struggled against its revelation to the end. His later work suffers from the attempt to impose optimism on a world clearly seen by cynical eyes. While the fools are revealed as mercilessly as ever and castigated as thoroughly in language and by devices of action, in the end they are accepted back into society, no better than they were before, because they are as good men as any available.

The lack of untainted characters is there as proof. Beaufort *(NI)*, lover of the Host's daughter, proves to be what Jonson's earlier work would have branded a mean-minded fortune hunter: he refuses to marry the woman he supposedly loves when he discovers her to be a poor inn-keeper's daughter. Expression of the same attitude constituted Angelo's first revelation of himself as an ignoble scoundrel *(CA)*; but when Beaufort, upon learning that the innkeeper is actually a wealthy nobleman, returns to his former ardor, he is welcomed with open arms and a mild admonition not to abandon his bride again. His shortcomings and Wittipol's are combined in the supposedly true lover Mr. Compasse *(ML)*, whose inclination toward Pleasance becomes an inclination toward marriage as soon as he discovers her to have been exchanged in the cradle with her supposed mistress; at the same time, he is capable of making bawdy puns about her in her presence. Representative of true nobility though she is, she functions in the play as a monetary and sexual object; her obvious dim-wittedness renders her, indeed, incapable of any higher role. She is much the same sort of woman as Awdrey in *Tale of a Tub*, only not so matrimonially avid; but Awdrey is made fun of by her creator, who holds up Pleasance as the best of a bad world. Placentia and the conspirators who attempt to pass her off, complete with damaged character, as Lady Loadstone's niece, are accepted back into society, without the slightest hint that they have reformed or even repented. They are what society is.

"If the men be naught, the times will be such" *(D,* 248), Jonson declared, and added confirmation to the possibility: "Now things daily fall: wits grow downe-ward, and *Eloquence* growes back-ward" *(D,* 921–22). He was not alone in his outlook. "Elizabethan satire and its satirist were but one part of a larger complex of philosophies, styles, reading tastes, and literary forms which had as their common center a renewed and increasingly pessimistic concern about such vital issues as the nature of man and the status of evil in the universal scheme."[4] The uniqueness of Jonson's view lies in his refusal to yield to pessimism on a metaphysical level, his insistence that "I cannot thinke *Nature* is so spent, and decay'd, that she can bring forth nothing worth her former yeares. . . . Men are decay'd, and *studies:* She is not" *(D,* 124–28).

4. Kernan, *Muse,* p. 243.

It is an insistence that helps to explain the determined cheerfulness of
the Host of the Light Heart, his obstinate desire that all those around him
shall live according to the emblem of his inn, while he explains to Lovel
that once, but no longer, the nursery of nobility

>   was noble,
> And only vertue made it, not the mercate,
> . . .
>   . . . goodnesse gave the greatnesse,
> And greatnesse worship: Every house became
> An Academy of honour, and those parts—
> We see departed, in the practise, now,
> Quite from the institution. *(NI,* I.3.52–59)

Jonson refuses to compromise on the value of the "institution." If things
daily fall, it is because men have fallen to unimagined depths:

> To play Sir *Pandarus* . . .
> And carry messages to Madam *Cresside.*
> Instead of backing the brave Steed, o'mornings,
> To mount the Chambermaid; and for a leape
> O'the vaulting horse, to play the vaulting house:
> For exercise of armes, a bale of dice,
> Or two or three packs of cards, to shew the cheat,
> And nimblenesse of hand: mistake a cloake
> From my Lords back, and pawne it . . .
> . . .
>   . . . These are the arts,
> Or seven liberall deadly sciences
> Of Pagery, or rather Paganisme,
> As the tides run. *(NI,* I.3.70–84)

These are the tides Jonson attempted to turn. In what was to be his
final effort, he sought inspiration from a world in which it might after
all be possible to show the spiritual ideal that sickened on the material
surfeit of the world around him. *The Sad Shepherd* represents no break in
the continuity of his writings, no sudden inexplicable turn from dramatic

to lyrical. It is the logical step of a man increasingly unable to find justification for his high ideals in the real world, toward the source of justification so often hinted at and even openly named before: the Golden Age.
Here the coin that had turned counterfeit might still ring true; here is
the mint of virtue. To make assurance doubly sure, Jonson adopted a
device (with its concomitant implications) to which he had never before
resorted: he removed the source of evil from man, to place it in a Witch.
She, with her son and daughter, cause the play's complications; all harm
is her offspring. A declaration of the power of love and mutual faith,
sounding in the outcome of *The Staple* and *The New Inn* like a wistful
hope, might become, in the prelapsarian world of *The Sad Shepherd,* a
convincing proclamation.

One wonders whether Jonson would have been able to carry the play
through to such an ending. Even in the fragment, the strain to see with
eyes innocent of corruption tells on the tone. Sympathy with the love-
stricken Amie is abruptly if momentarily shattered by her attempt to
find a comparison for her pain: "I often have been torne with thorne and
briar;/ Both in the Leg, and Foot, and somewhat higher" *(SS,* II.4.21–22).
It is the same sort of unintentional innuendo that condemns the senti-
ments of dupes in the great plays. Similarly, extravagance and total self-involvement, sure signs of irrational and blameworthy humors, spill out in
every speech of the bereaved shepherd of the title. Even the pastoral
world contains the wrongheaded, if not the wicked. It contains those who
can be worked upon by evil—contains the seeds of its own destruction,
as the prelapsarian world always does.

Jonson is too honest, too clear-eyed a fox with regard to practical truth,
to blink the facts. Man will always fall again; man is made to fall. Yet
Jonson was also, in the face of the world around him, too stubbornly a
hedgehog to relinquish his vision of man as potentially godlike, of a plan
originally divine, though his view necessarily reduced whatever reality
was put beside it (even the Golden Age) to imperfection which demanded
satire. The combination of vision and judgment makes of his plays great
works.

Selected Bibliography

Barish, Jonas A., *Ben Jonson and the Language of Prose Comedy*, Cambridge, Mass., Harvard University Press, 1960.

Baskervill, C. R., *English Elements in Jonson's Early Comedy*, Austin, University of Texas Press, 1911.

Baum, Helena Watts, *The Satiric and the Didactic in Ben Jonson's Comedy*, Chapel Hill, University of North Carolina Press, 1947.

Campbell, O. J., *Comicall Satyre and Shakespeare's Troilus and Cressida*, San Marino (Los Angeles, Printed by the Adcraft Press), 1938.

Coleridge, Samuel Taylor, *Coleridge's Literary Criticism*, ed. J. W. Mackail, London, Henry Frowde, 1908.

———, *Coleridge's Miscellaneous Criticism*, ed. Thomas Middleton Raysor, Cambridge, Mass., Harvard University Press, 1936.

Dryden, John, *Essays of John Dryden*, W. P. Ker, ed., Oxford, The Clarendon Press, 1900.

Einstein, Lewis, *The Italian Renaissance in England*, New York, Columbia University Press, 1902.

Eliot, T. S., "Ben Jonson," in *Elizabethan Essays*, London, Faber and Faber, 1934.

Enck, John J., *Jonson and the Comic Truth*, Madison, University of Wisconsin Press, 1957.

Hilberry, Clarence B., *Ben Jonson's Ethics in Relation to Stoic and Humanist Ethical Thought,* Chicago, University of Chicago Press, 1933.

Hinze, Otto, *Studien zu Ben Jonsons Namengebung in seinen Dramen,* Leipzig, Thomas and Hubert (for the University of Leipzig), 1919.

Jonson, Benjamin, *Ben Jonson,* ed. C. H. Herford and Percy and Evelyn Simpson, 11 vols. Oxford, The Clarendon Press, 1925–52.

Judson, Alexander Corbin, ed., *Cynthia's Revels,* Yale Studies in English, 45, New York, Henry Holt, 1912.

Kernan, Alvin, *The Cankered Muse,* Yale Studies in English, 142, New Haven, Yale University Press, 1959.

Knights, L. C., *Drama and Society in the Age of Jonson,* London, Chatto and Windus, 1937.

Mallory, Herbert S., ed., *Poetaster,* Yale Studies in English, 27, New York, Henry Holt, 1905.

Partridge, Edward B., *The Broken Compass,* New York, Columbia University Press, 1958.

Penniman, Josiah Harmar, *The War of the Theatres,* Boston, Ginn, 1897.

Rhys, Ernest, ed., *Ben Jonson,* New York, American Book Co., 1915.

Sackton, A. H., *Rhetoric as a Dramatic Language in Ben Jonson,* New York, Columbia University Press, 1948.

Selin, William Edward, ed., *The Case Is Altered,* Yale Studies in English, 56, New Haven, Yale University Press, 1917.

Sidney, Sir Philip, *Defence of Poesy,* ed. Albert S. Cook, Boston, Ginn, 1890.

Small, Roscoe Addison, *The Stage-Quarrel between Ben Jonson and the So-Called Poetasters,* Breslau, M. and H. Marcus, 1899.

Swinburne, Algernon Charles, *A Study of Ben Jonson,* New York, Worthington, 1889.

Upton, James, *Remarks on Three Plays of Benjamin Jonson,* London, G. Hawkins, 1749.

Waith, Eugene M., "The Poet's Morals in Jonson's *Poetaster,*" *Modern Language Quarterly, 12* (March 1951), 13–19.

Woodbridge, Elisabeth, *Studies in Jonson's Comedy,* New York, Lamson, Wolffe, 1898.

Index

89504

DATE DUE

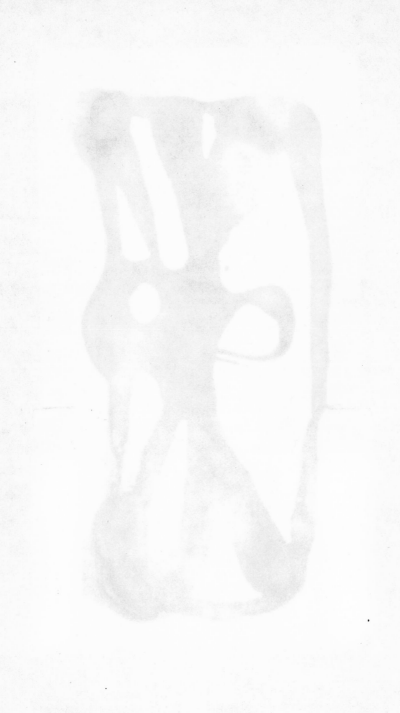